early interpreters, especially Hannah Aren
Theodor Adorno, challenged his seriousne
originality by allud'

Hot Property

Françoise Meltzer

Hot Property

*The Stakes and Claims of
Literary Originality*

THE UNIVERSITY OF CHICAGO PRESS

Chicago and London

FRANÇOISE MELTZER is professor in the Department of Romance Languages and Literatures, the Committee on Comparative Studies in Literature, and the College, University of Chicago. She is the author of *Salome and the Dance of Writing: Portraits of Mimesis in Literature* (1987), editor of *The Trial(s) of Psychoanalysis* (1987, 1988), and translator of Georges Poulet's *Exploding Poetry: Baudelaire/Rimbaud* (1984), all published by the University of Chicago Press.

The University of Chicago Press, Chicago 60637
The University of Chicago Press, Ltd., London
© 1994 by The University of Chicago
All rights reserved. Published 1994
Printed in the United States of America

03 02 01 00 99 98 97 96 95 94   1 2 3 4 5

ISBN: 0-226-51975-9 (cloth)

Library of Congress Cataloging-in-Publication Data

Meltzer, Françoise.
    Hot property : the stakes and claims of literary originality /
Françoise Meltzer.
        p.   cm.
    Includes bibliographical references (p.) and index.
    1. Originality in literature.—2. Authorship.   3. Authorship—Sex
differences.   4. Literature—Philosophy.   I. Title.
PN166.M45   1994
801—dc20   93-6275
                                                          CIP

po mo mai
lo fino
lo bello bello
lo tant aimado
lo martolando

This morning I am in a sort of temper, indolent and supremely careless. . . . If I had teeth of pearl and the breath of lilies I should call it languor, but as I am I must call it laziness. In this state of effeminacy the fibres of the brain are relaxed in common with the rest of the body.

JOHN KEATS, *letter to his brother and sister, March 1819.*

CONTENTS

ACKNOWLEDGMENTS

I WANT ABOVE ALL to thank my graduate students at the University of Chicago, who continue to be my most demanding (although patient) teachers. In particular, thanks are owed to Frank Rothchild and Michael Salda and to several of my students who became research assistants at varying points in this project. Their high standards and intelligence kept me (mostly) honest: Jessica Berman, John Chaimov, Nancy Henry, Margaret Jewett, Maureen McLane, Laura Mueller, and David Schabes.

My gratitude as well to my friends David Grene, Harry Harootunian, Marie-Hélène Huet, Stephen Melville, Nicholas Rubinfier, and Michael Steinberg, for helping me to focus my thinking and to recast some of the discussion. The book has been improved a great deal by their comments and suggestions, as it has by my superb editor, Alan Thomas.

Yves Bonnefoy generously gave of his time and insights; I am honored by the friendship he has shown me. A particular note of thanks to Irwin Rubin, my brother-in-law, who gave me a computer and thus delivered me from the fate of being the last academic still wielding scissors and tape. And to Marie-Claude Rubin, for getting born in the midst of this project, thus delaying and enriching it immeasurably.

The University of Chicago generously offered me a year's leave from teaching, which allowed me to complete this study.

Finally, I need to mention the constant intellectual guidance, tolerance, and support of a few close friends: Manfred Hoppe, who did not live to see this project completed but who is present throughout its pages (as throughout my life); Ziva Ben-Porat; David Tracy; and (as always, especially) Bernard Rubin.

INTRODUCTION

IT WAS MONTAIGNE who noted that all knowledge is public property. But such a statement rests upon the assumption of the alternative, private property, which Rousseau sees as the cause of every major disaster to befall human society. Beware, writes Rousseau in the *Discourse on the Origin of Inequality,* of the imposter who would have you believe that property can be private. You are lost "if you forget that the fruit belongs to everyone, and the earth to no one." Originality is already implicated here: within the literary establishment, any claim of originality seeks to protect its fruits as being (on) private property. If no one else has thought quite the same thought, nor written it down in the same way, then the thought and its fruit, the text, must be protected—so, at least, runs the logic. The trouble (one of many) is that an idea cannot be owned since it partakes of human thought and language, which belong to everyone. And so we are back to Montaigne.

This book takes glancing blows at the notion of literary originality and how it understands itself. It is a study that grew out of my first book, *Salome and the Dance of Writing,* which examined assumptions about representation in literature. Here I am treating moments of misrepresentation—either real or imagined—or, perhaps more accurately, moments in literature when the claim to originality is either threatened (Freud reading Descartes), overtly attacked (Celan, when accused of plagiarism), displaced (Willy signing his name to Colette's writings), or domesticated (certain interpretations of Walter Benjamin). Each case study signals a moment when "originality" itself as a construct, or even as a mythology, risks being destabilized, or uncovered as the greater fraud underlying the immediate one. This book is not, therefore, about the history of these cases, although it certainly is embedded in the historical contexts informing them. Nor is it about copyright law, which has been amply, and brilliantly, treated by others.[1]

1. Two of the more recent and helpful examples are Mark Rose's study "The Author as Proprietor: *Donaldson v. Becket* and the Genealogy of Modern Author-

1

What I am trying, obliquely, to get at is the place and role of a Western, First World, masculinist literary criticism that has itself at stake when it articulates two principles: first, that great literature is "original," and, second, that only literary criticism itself is in a position to judge what is and what is not original, to what extent a given work is original, and how successful a work is. Moreover, literary criticism reserves the right to alter the canon. The two most infamous examples of demotion from the constellation of literary greats are Chatterton and MacPherson.

MacPherson is of particular interest here since his *Ossian* was a forgery, not a theft, and was by literary lights in fact "original." The influence of *Ossian* upon literature is as undeniable (Werther, to give one of the more important examples, reads from *Ossian* shortly before killing himself), as it is upon translation theory. Yet when it was discovered that MacPherson had largely invented a Scottish national epic, rather than having edited existing manuscripts and songs of such an epic, he and his warrior bard were instantly thrown out of the literary pantheon.[2]

Conversely, Norman Fruman and others have spent a great deal of time and effort demonstrating beyond doubt that Coleridge was a literary thief.[3] The amount of resistance generated by such studies is to me far more intriguing than any speculation

ship, *Representations* 23 (Summer 1988):51-85, and Susan Stewart's *Crimes of Writing: Problems in the Containment of Representation* (New York and Oxford, 1991).

2. On this and other forgeries, see Anthony Grafton's highly informative (and often hilarious) *Forgers and Critics: Creativity and Duplicity in Western Scholarship* (Princeton, 1990). See also *The Forger's Art: Forgery and the Philosophy of Art*, ed. Denis Dutton (Berkeley and Los Angeles, 1983). One essay in that volume, by Hope B. Werness, deals with the case of van Meegeren, who temporarily succeeded in fooling people that his paintings were lost Vermeers. The case of Meegeren demonstrates how similar issues (originality, authenticity) manifest themselves in alternate contexts—here, painting and art historians' grip on painting. The Meegeren forgeries point as well to the blindness of an era to its fashions: Meegeren's "Vermeers" are clearly typed by German Expressionism; Vermeer is seen through the lens of the 1930s, a fact which was "invisible" at the time he painted. Also see Nelson Goodman's *Languages of Art* (Indianpolis, 1976) for a good discussion on the stakes of forgery; and Ian Haywood, *Faking It: Art and the Politics of Forgery* (New York, 1987). For literary forgery in the Slavic tradition, as well as the importance of translation poetics and of Ossian, I have drawn on an unpublished essay by Franticek Svejkovsky.

3. The following (to name but the most obvious) have leveled claims of grand larceny in Coleridge: Thomas De Quincey, *Recollections of the Lakes and the Lake Poets* (Harmondsworth, U.K., 1970); J. C. Ferrier, "The Plagiarisms of S. T. Coleridge," *Blackwood's Magazine* 47 (March 1840); the editorial notes of T. M. Raysor in

about (or even answer to) why Coleridge stole in the first place. So, too, Stendhal plagiarized "his" first three works, and criticism similarly rushes to explain, excuse, or hotly deny. "How can you be a plagiarist if you don't sign your name," Stendhal grumbled when accused (entirely accurately) of stealing wholesale from a Señor Carpani in order to produce *Haydn, Mozart, and Metastase*.[4] Robert Alter and Carol Cosman generously venture the theory that this was Stendhal's way of overcoming a serious case of writer's block.[5] Romain Rolland's preface to the 1914 edition of *Haydn* (p. li) tries to reassure by claiming that Stendhal's supporters believe he was original in his ability elegantly to transform other people's thoughts (an excuse which, as is said in French, smells of sweat). On the other hand, putting others' prose into a new context is the raison d'être of allusion, which, unlike plagiarism, banks on the reader's memory. Rolland himself concludes, a bit sadly, that Stendhal's real mistake (which, Rolland reminds us, he shared with Chateaubriand) was in omitting his sources. Once again, what concerns me here is what the literary-critical stakes are, what is being protected. Whether or why a theft occurred is not at issue.

As any study on originality will attest, the fear of plagiarism (a

Shakespearean Criticism and of J. Shaweron in *Bibliographia Literaria*, ed. G. Watson (Everyman Library); Anna Augusta von Helmholtz's "The Indebtedness of Samuel Taylor Coleridge to August Wilhelm von Schlegel" (Madison, WI, B.A. thesis, 1907); René Wellek, *A History of Modern Criticism, 1750–1950*, vol. 1 (New Haven, 1955)—downright hostile; Molly Lefebure, *Samuel Taylor Coleridge: A Bondage of Opium* (London, 1974); Thomas McFarland, *Coleridge and the Pantheist Tradition* (New York, 1969); and the most notorious, Norman Fruman, *Coleridge, the Damaged Archangel* (New York, 1971). Fruman and others have discovered that Wordsworth gave Coleridge some of his discarded poems so that his friend would have something to show for his "genius."

   4. "Un anonyme peut-il être un plagiaire?" See *Vies de Haydn, de Mozart et de Métastase*, ed. Daniel Muller; Romain Rolland, introduction to *Oeuvres complètes de Stendhal*, ed. Edouard Champion (Paris, 1914). The Haydn part of this was taken from Giuseppe Carpani, an Italian who had just published the life of that composer. Stendhal apparently backdated his own translation, which posed as an original work, so that when the Italian author wrote to him to complain of plagiarism, Stendhal indignantly turned the accusation around onto the hapless (and livid) Señor Carpani. The Mozart portion was lifted from a biographical article by C. Winkler; the Métastase part "leaned" on an article in Italian by a Giuseppe Baretti and J-.C-.L. Sismondi. For a brilliant and affectionate treatment of Stendhal's obsession with masks and pseudonyms, see Jean Starobinski, "Stendhal pseudonyme," in *L'Oeil vivant* (Paris, 1961), 193–257.

   5. *A Lion for Love: A Critical Biography of Stendhal* (Cambridge, MA, 1986).

frequently well-founded anxiety and a symptom of originality) does not suddenly appear in the eighteenth century. The Greeks, the Romans, the writers of the Renaissance, seventeenth-century Europeans—all worried about having their ideas stolen. When Rousseau in his *Confessions* splinters into shards of paranoia, accusing everyone of stealing from him (his ideas, his fame, his good reputation, his texts), he is not reflecting a new sensibility born of the preromantics; rather, he is echoing an anxiety which has always, to some degree, been in place. This anxiety is grounded in the idea of creating a sovereign textual subject, one which purports to double mimetically the authoritative and self-contained subjectivity of the author.

The cult of the individual, then, and its concomitant insistence on uniqueness are at work long before the rise of the bourgeoisie and are implicit in any originary economy. The early European romantics (Friedrich von Schlegel, Novalis, Wackenroder, and Tieck in Germany; Coleridge and Wordsworth in England) did, however, articulate the notion of "original genius," which, as several scholars have noted, complicated things immensely if only because the great literati were required to demonstrate both originality and genius in spontaneous and utterly convincing ways recognizable only to literary criticism. What emerges in the requirements for greatness in literary authorship is a paradox: the demand for spontaneous creativity on the one hand (proof of natural "genius"), and a work ethic that insists upon earning acquired goods or status on the other. Novalis's Heinrich von Ofterdingen never writes a line, but he is a recognized poet because he has a poetic sensibility. The antibildungsroman that bears his name argues against the hard-working apprenticeship to civic responsibility exemplified by Goethe's Wilhelm Meister. Laziness becomes the other possible side of the genius coin, and by the end of the nineteenth century the accusation of indolence an easy swipe by a European culture grown impatient with degenerate ways. Thus does the bourgeoisie attack its own cult of individuality when it is vested in a *fainéant*, a *Taugenichts*, a ne'er-do-well. Is Mallarmé an original genius, eking out his great poetry at the expense of his nerves and mind (an echo of the composer Berglinger, for example, the episode which closes the anonymous, early romantic German work *Herzensergiessungen*)? Or is he a decadent, useless member of society, which he parasitically saps for his own purposes, hiding under the mask of genius? I neither answer nor, indeed, directly address these questions here, but their stakes for the machinery of literary criticism (machinery that grinds in this critical work as well, I am afraid) are what concern this study.

The accusation of plagiarism today is a grave one in many fields. In politics it seems particularly deadly, as if we expected our "leaders" to display the same creativity as the "founding fathers" (a metaphor, needless to say, for originality). We should remind ourselves that John F. Kennedy's *Profiles in Courage,* which gives portraits of such "fathers," was itself ghostwritten, and was thus not by Kennedy at all, an irony that seems to undermine his anticipated place (at the time of the publication) in the chain of forefathers. The cover of the *New Republic* of April 10, 1988, proclaims a "Culture of Plagiarism," by which it means ghostwriters (Casper the friendly ghost is sitting at the typewriter). The arts world is divided by high-tech alterations of sights and sounds; computers can simulate "authentic" video and media events. People can lose the legal rights to their own names, as did, for example, the designer Halston, who sold the rights to his name only to see it thereafter applied to everything from rugs to mittens. The *New York Times,* in an article of cryonics, can ask, "If you duplicate and store yourself as a backup copy, is that copy you?" (January 20, 1989). Meanwhile, mice are patented, spleens are copied, and freelance artists, it is ruled, retain the copyright to a work of art as long as they are not in a "conventional" employment situation with the person who commissioned said work.

While it is no surprise that a culture of late capitalism should be so obsessed about the limits and boundaries of private property, we seem to be increasingly haunted by an odd anxiety every time the idea of originality is at issue. Jacques Derrida in particular has shown the extent to which we are wedded, in our Western metaphysical tradition, to the importance of beginnings, of originary status, of first over second, of breath over text. Our culture is dominated by myths of discovery (America, electricity, the telephone, the atomic bomb); and of being first (George Washington is father to the first First World country). While these issues will not be raised directly in the pages that follow, they are symptoms of the same anxiety: it is not a fear of influence (although certainly that is part of it), but stems rather from the insistence on the new, the creative, the true. Underlying these convictions is another series of beliefs: in the individual and his—and I mean *his*—sovereignty; in a patriarchal hegemony as dominating culture and metaphysics; in a concomitant feminine economy as eternally secondary, unable by definition to partake of an originary model; in private property and the exclusionary systems that ensue; in manual work as a valid labor and product, to which writing remains a destabilized and ambiguous correlative. Is writing work? Is it "really" manual work, and, if so, can its product, the text, be owned by the laborer?

Finally and inevitably, the belief in originality and the possessiveness it entails engender the prose and economy of paranoia: paranoia in the "creators," whose fear of being robbed masks a more basic anxiety that originality may be impossible and illusory; and paranoia in the scaffolding that arises and supports itself by [means of] those creators—criticism (or theory) itself. Criticism can exist largely because of such an illusion and is therefore (unconsciously, for the most part) determined to keep it alive, demonstrating in its own efforts at originality or the new that it shares in more than a practical fashion the mythology it seeks to analyze. There are moments when anxiety about originality or about origin risks exposing the fraud it noisily conceals. The present study focuses on some of these moments, and the destabilization of a critical discourse and ontology they fleetingly reveal.

Finally, a word about the way in which this book is written. The style is inductive, for lack of a better word. This is a conscious choice on my part, an *après coup* technique that I hope will underscore my attempt to destabilize certain well-known notions concerning originality. The notes, besides their bibliographic function, are intended as sub- and (sometimes) even countertexts. This admittedly taxing strategy is meant to serve as a textual echo of the problems with which I am grappling. So too I place apparently unrelated events and analyses side by side with little obvious rationale and frequently abrupt transitions in the hope that the disconnected events will reveal themselves as the multi-faceted symptomology of the same disease. Thus one can accuse my prose of a willed economy of hysteria that mirrors its subject matter: literary symptoms are produced that initially dissimulate the veritable problem, displacing its origin. But such a displacement is, I believe, the motivating malady of literature, one that literary criticism and theory are condemned to mime with parallel symptoms of their own. What emerges gradually in this study is the argument that the pursuit of originality, the fear of being robbed of a "new" idea, the drive to be first, even the work ethic itself are symptoms of a gendered theology of origin.

C H A P T E R

1

Freud and Descartes:
Dreaming On

Que ce qui est passion au regard d'un sujet
est toujours action à quelque autre égard.

—DESCARTES

O N NOVEMBER 10, 1619, Descartes was twenty-three
years old and in Germany. A few months earlier he had
witnessed the crowning of the emperor Ferdinand and
signed up for the duke of Bavaria's army. As early as April 23
in the same year, Descartes was writing to Isaac Beeckman of
tremendous mental activity: "My mind," he wrote, "is already
traveling." On November 10, his brain is "on fire." His goal is to
"distinguish the true from the false, to cast aside all prejudice."[1]
It is a day of great joy, during which, it seems, he makes no mention of God. What followed is legendary: the three consecutive
dreams Descartes had in the night, which were to become the
foundation of his philosophy. For the dreams revealed an "admi-

This chapter is an expanded and revised version of "Descartes' Dreams and
Freud's Failure, or the Politics of Originality," in *The Trial(s) of Psychoanalysis*, ed.
Françoise Meltzer (Chicago, 1987, 1988), pp. 81–102. ©1987, 1988, by The Uni-
versity of Chicago.

1. All three quotations are cited by Georges Poulet in his "Le Songe de Descartes," *Etudes sur le temps humain*, 4 vols. (Paris, 1949–68), 1:65–66; my translation. I refer the reader here and throughout this discussion on Descartes to a
"narration" of the dreams, given in the appendix to this chapter. I have taken
this "narration" from Lewis S. Feuer's unswerving psychoanalytic reading, "The
Dreams of Descartes," *American Imago* 20 (Spring 1963): 3–26. For a complete text
of the dreams in English, see Norman Kemp Smith, *New Studies in the Philosophy
of Descartes: Descartes as Pioneer* (London, 1952), pp. 33–39. The French text is in
Oeuvres de Descartes, 13 vols., ed. Charles Adam and Paul Tannery (Paris, 1908–
13), 10:180–88.

rable science" to Descartes. They were important, moreover, not only intellectually and spiritually. After those dreams, as Descartes wrote to his friend Balzac twelve years later, in sleep "I experience all the pleasures imagined in the Fables, I mix insensibly my reveries of the day with those of the night."[2] Until the three dreams, Descartes's nights were filled with phantoms; after them, he claimed never to have had a nightmare again.

In terms of the Western metaphysical tradition, of course, those dreams are equally astonishing: they are the *cause* of what Hegel (in his famous text on Descartes) called a revolution of the mind which marks the beginning of modern Western philosophy, a revolution born of three dreams. In terms of Descartes's own psychic life, further, these dreams herald a birth into health and productivity; they usher in the confident, mature Descartes. Not only do they allow him to sleep henceforth, and to sleep peacefully; they also, according to their author, rid him of the pallor and dry cough that he claimed he had received from his mother, who had died of a lung ailment. The dreams, then, free him from the mother's lingering legacy, her disease imposed, phantomlike, upon the son.[3] Thus, as a number of critics have noted, the end of bad health and the occurrence of the dreams essentially coincide. We will return to the significance of this point later. For now, however, it is important to remember that the creation of what is acknowledged to be a "new" way of thinking engenders a Descartes who is healthy—or at least sees himself so—in every way.

An entire philosophy inspired by dreams; a self-cure emerging

---

2. "Le sommeil où j'éprouve tous les plaisirs qui sont imaginés dans les fables, je mêle insensiblement mes rêveries du jour avec celles da la nuit." *Descartes: Oeuvres et lettres*, ed. André Bridoux (Paris, 1953), p. 941. The English translation is cited by Feuer, "The Dreams of Descartes," p. 22.

3. In a letter to Princess Elizabeth, Descartes says: "For, having been born of a mother who died a few days after my birth of a lung ailment, caused by unhappiness, I had inherited from her a dry cough and a pale complexion, which I kept until I was over twenty years of age." ("Car, étant né d'une mère qui mourut, peu de jours après ma naissance, d'un mal de poumon, causé par quelques déplaisirs, j'avais hérité d'elle une toux sèche, et une couleur pâle, que j'ai gardeé jusques à l'âge de plus de vingt ans." *Oeuvres et lettres*, p. 1188; my translation. I am using the notion of the phantom particularly in Nicolas Abraham's sense. See his essay "Notes on the Phantom," trans. Nicholas T. Rand, in Meltzer, *The Trial(s) of Psychoanalysis*, pp. 75–80.

as the unexpected side effect; a revolution in thought—surely such an event prefigures, almost as if in resonant preparation, Freud's own finding. Freud, who himself calls his psychoanalysis a "discovery," also dubs it a philosophy, despite his well-known protestations against philosophers and their works. Moreover, although his "discovery" of repression bears a striking resemblance to Schopenhauer's idea of insanity, Freud claims that he himself had not read that philosopher: "The theory of repression," he writes firmly, "quite certainly came to me independently of any other source; I know of no outside impression which might have suggested it to me." For a long time, he continues, he had thought this idea to be "entirely original"; but upon being shown a passage from *The World as Will and Idea,* Freud concluded, "Once again I owe the chance of making a discovery to my not being well-read. Yet others have read the passage and passed it by without making this discovery." Therefore, says Freud, in a less-than-convincing manner, "[I] forgo all claims to priority in the many instances in which laborious psychoanalytic investigation can merely confirm the truths which the philosophers recognized by intuition."[4] It is no coincidence that analysis "labors" to attain a truth, while philosophy stumbles upon it. Freud is obliquely insisting upon the scientific (and therefore methodical and truth-bearing) character of psychoanalysis and, simultaneously, upon the aleatoric (and therefore unreliable) character of philosophy.

The extent to which priority, and thus originality, are troublesome issues for Freud here is clear from the vocabulary choice in the passages just cited: "discovery" and "came to me independently" clash rather seriously with the modest promise to "forgo all claims to priority" and to abdicate the notion of being "entirely original." The defensive assurance that the notion of "repression" is his own discovery, caused by "no *outside* impression," seeks to establish that the idea emerged from *inside* Freud alone and is thus his own creation, regardless of what others are thinking and writing at the same time.

On the one hand, priority, as Freud would have it, has no mo-

4. Sigmund Freud, *On the History of the Psycho-Analytic Movement.* In *The Standard Edition of the Complete Psychological Works of Sigmund Freud,* ed. and trans. James Strachey, 24 vols. (London, 1953–74), 14:15–16.

nopoly on originality if a "creator" can claim ignorance ("Once again I owe the chance of making a discovery to my not being well-read"). This same assurance is at odds with the bow to philosophy, a bow with which Freud appears to be collaborating with famous philosophers in exploring the unknown. But the second statement, that of relinquishing "all claims to priority," has already been thrown into question by Freud's previous insistence upon having priority. So, on the other hand, priority is useful if it can be claimed unequivocally.

It should be remembered in this regard that the terms "inside" and "outside" have a complex history with respect to inspiration. In the West, inspiration comes mainly from the "outside" (visits from gods, demons, prophetic dreams, and, of course, genies) until the organicist myths that spawned early romanticism. The organicists (such as Shaftesbury, Young, and, later, Schelling) argue that genius is like a seed, impounding its own substance; all the material is already there, inside, and needs only the proper watering to unfold. This move from the outside to the inside is mirrored at the linguistic level: in the latter part of the eighteenth century, in German, French, and English, for example, one begins to *be* a genius rather than to *have* genius. Freud's insistence that his ideas come from *inside* him, with no outside influence, is a demonstration of the romantic legacy and the way it modifies the topography of originality and, consequently, language.[5]

Later in the passage we have been considering, Freud informs us that he has "denied" himself "the very great pleasure of reading the work of Nietzsche" so as to avoid "being hampered" by any sort of "anticipatory idea." Here again, originality is protected by ignorance when similarities are found between great minds. The ambivalent status of priority (or Freud's double standard in his interpretation of it) is a particularly thorny issue for Freud in relation to philosophy. The situation becomes even more delicate when it concerns a "discovery" by one Descartes, who is called, after all, "the father of modern philos-

---

5. See, for example, M. H. Abrams, *The Mirror and the Lamp: Romantic Theory and the Critical Tradition* (Oxford, 1971), which remains, I think, one of the best works on the issue of romanticism and its notions of genius. See too Eric Blackall's *The Emergence of German as a Literary Language, 1700–1775* (Ithaca, NY, 1959).

ophy." Freud has no wish to inherit, to be derivative, or to echo. His wish is to create; to be the origin; to be the father, not the son; to be "entirely original."[6]

It is intriguing to consider, in this light, the fantasy plaque Freud imagines on the house where he had the dream of Irma's Injection (as with Descartes, a kind of "specimen dream"): "In this House, on July 24th, 1895, the Secret of Dreams was Revealed to Dr. Sigm. Freud."[7] By the time Freud writes this to Wilhelm Fliess, the history of Western philosophy has long since hung a plaque on its own house, and it reads something like this: "In this place, on November 11, 1619, the secret of three dreams was revealed to René Descartes." But Freud, as will be shown later, expressed no real interest in these "specimen" dreams of Descartes's—none at all. Such a lack of interest is by far the most curious aspect of the entire sequence; yet few critics have remarked on it. It is as if Freud's feigned indifference to Descartes's dreams had been donned, like so many green glasses, by everybody else.

Freud emphasizes the word "discovery"—revealing, as we have noted, his well-documented obsession with originality and (which must follow) with possession, or ownership. The same holds true, however, for Descartes, who also struggles with the problem of the original, of discovery. His obsession with authorship (first rights, priority, originality) manifested itself particularly in his relationship with his friend Beeckman, whom he suspected of stealing his ideas.[8] Freud, in other words, is not merely the product of a postromantic age with its emphasis on original

6. For a convincing argument that Freud's lack of interest in philosophy "protest[s] too much," see Stanley Cavell's "Psychoanalysis and Cinema: The Melodrama of the Unknown Woman," in Meltzer, *The Trial(s) of Psychoanalysis*, pp. 227–58.

7. Freud, *The Interpretation of Dreams*, in *The Standard Edition*, 4:121, n. 1; further references to *Interpretation*, abbreviated *ID*, will be included in the text. The passage is from a letter to Fliess of June 12, 1900. Descartes himself frequently uses a house metaphor to describe his philosophy, which he says calls for the demolition of the old house of thought in order to permit the building of a new house, complete with a new foundation. See, e.g., the second part of the *Discourse* in *Oeuvres et lettres*, p. 134. See too the opening to the *Meditations*, ibid., p. 267.

8. See, e.g., Ben-Ami Scharfstein, who notes that Descartes was afraid of losing things but also of "losing his ideas to others." "Descartes' Dreams," *Philosophical Forum* 1 (Spring 1969): 293–317.

genius and creativity. Descartes manifests some of the same assumptions (and thus paranoia) toward his friends and correspon-
dents; he is afraid of being robbed. But if such an obsession with
originality begins long before the writings of a Friedrich Schlegel
or a Schelling, it is when that obsession is combined with a given
historical situation that it truly takes hold. Descartes, like Freud,
has nagging doubts about the political implications of his stance,
but for the French philosopher those doubts turn on the possibility of recantation and on the authority of the Church.

Before we continue with Freud's struggles, let us look first at
Descartes's famous dreams. A few comments about the manuscript are in order here: the three consecutive dreams were written down by Descartes in Latin, in his own words. Adrien Baillet,
Descartes's highly deferential biographer, possessed this Latin
manuscript, the "Olympica," which has since been lost. Thus we
cannot compare Baillet's paraphrasing of Descartes's rendition to
the original. We have, unfortunately, only Baillet's summary and
translation into French.[9] Occasionally, Baillet gives the original
Latin, but those instances are rare. And since we are here working from an English text, we have the translation of a translation
to the third power: the translation of the dreams into language;
the translation of the Latin into French, further transmuted by
paraphrase; and, finally, the French put into English, with the
text again abridged. The result is a sort of exaggerated secondary
process, manifest at both textual and psychological (Descartes
himself, then Baillet) levels. Baillet's text reads exactly like the
biographies (or saints' lives, not an unimportant analogy in Baillet's case, as we shall see) that Sartre pokes fun at in *The Words.*
Seemingly trivial or at least obscure incidents are given enormous
weight in light of the fact that the protagonist is later revealed to
be a "genius." Baillet and the reader wink at each other or jointly
wring their hands as the young soldier Descartes struggles to become the great man we already know he will succeed in becoming. The manuscript of the dreams thus presents obstacles to a
close reading. These transmutations and reinterpretations may

9. We also have Leibnitz's notes taken from the "Olympica"; he had no interest
in the dreams but was concerned, rather, with mathematical proofs.

partly explain Freud's disinterest, although, as we will see later, Freud's own theories are useful in undoing precisely this type of textual and psychic overinterpretation.

On the day of the dreams, Baillet tells us, Descartes had "decided to put aside all prejudice, to render the mind naked." A spiritual ardor left him only with "a great love for the truth." The past was severed. Let us retain the notion of the mind rendered naked (*son imagination lui presentat son esprit tout nud*);[10] for now, however, let us consider the severance with the past. Baillet's vocabulary describing this day of intense intellectual joy and frenzy is one of illumination: he uses such words as fever, ardor, light, fire, enthusiasm. These words prepare the way for the dark and frightening night which follows. The severance with the past is in a sense prefigured by the contrast between the joyous day and the night with its dark dreams and ensuing doubts.

It is significant that the first dream having to do with the difficulty of walking upright, gives Descartes a metaphor for the second part of his *Discourse on Method*: to walk with assurance in darkness, the philosopher tells us, one must walk slowly to avoid falling.[11] This first dream is traditionally read as an attempt to return to the past: the college on the road, with its retreat and remedy for sickness, is the desire for the college of La Flèche, where Descartes had spent happy years. The dream, like the *Discourse*, uses the metaphor of walking. Again in the third part of the *Discourse*, Descartes notes that his thought will not imitate "travelers lost in a wood [who] wander about." It will rather learn to walk in a straight line, to go to the end of a given path before giving it up.[12] The motif of walking in circles, or failing to walk upright in a straight line, becomes the metaphor in the

10. Adrien Baillet, *La Vie de Monsieur Descartes*, 2 vols. (Paris, 1691), 1:80.

11. "Mais, comme un homme qui marche seul et dans les ténèbres, je me résolus d'aller si lentement et d'user de tant de circonspection en toutes choses, que si je n'avançais que fort peu, je me garderais bien au moins de tomber." Descartes, *Discours*, in *Oeuvres et lettres*, p. 136. Here again, Freud and Descartes, to explain their methodology, share the metaphor of walking over unknown terrain. Descartes uses this analogy in the *Discourse*, and Freud uses it primarily in the opening of *The Interpretation of Dreams*.

12. Descartes, *Discourse*, in *Philosophical Writings*, ed. and trans. Elizabeth Anscombe and Peter Thomas Geach (1954; London, 1969), p. 25; see *Oeuvres et lettres*, p. 142.

philosophical works for the difficulty of maintaining a logical, linear progression of thought. Prejudice is an ever-present lure,
which leads thought in circles so that it behaves like travelers
lost in the forest. The geometrical notion of the advantage of the
straight line—that it is the shortest distance between two
points—is directly applied by Descartes to the *méthode* he is pre-
paring. The *steps* of the *méthode* are grounded in linearity, which
functions first as an analogy (the lost traveler cannot attain a
straight trajectory). But the analogy quickly becomes a metaphor
for thought itself, and for the only way to arrive at truth.

But walking on one side also becomes a metaphor for the division between body and mind, and between the new and the old
Descartes: between the one who likes his life of debauchery, as
he was later to call it, and the one who is demanding an existence
dedicated to the life of the mind. But this now famous cleavage
between body and mind which the dream seems to inaugurate
also suggests a different split: that of the subject from itself. "It
does not follow," Descartes was to write later, "that I must now
be that which I have been before." I am speaking here not of the
"old" and "new" sides of Descartes but rather of the subject (what
Hegel would call consciousness) realizing itself as an autonomous
though ever-changing entity. As Georges Poulet notes, this dream
says that only the present exists. The past (the phantoms, the
college) and the future (the inability to walk forward, in a straight
line) are closed.[13] Within that present, the subject is constantly
looking at itself as its own double.

One can already sense the beginnings of the problem that
Freud was to take up, in the manner of Descartes: "Wo Es war,
soll Ich werden." In this statement by Freud there is first the assumption of what Poulet calls the cogito's *dédoublement de l'être*.
Because no step is possible except by virtue of the preceding one,
Descartes's linear logic already entails a doubling of the self, and
thus, contrary to what is usually seen as the triumph of the subject, puts into question the stability of that subject (though not,
of course, its existence).

The whirlwind in the first dream suggests the traditional way

13. See Poulet, "Le Songe de Descartes," pp. 72–73.

by which God speaks to man (in Job, for example, God speaks "out of the tempest"). And in this tradition, the wind acts as the breath and spirit of God. It is impetuous: Leibnitz cites the "Olympica" as referring to the *ventus spiritum.* But the whirlwind is also an evil genius, pushing Descartes violently up against the Church. Here again, we have the Latin: *a malo spiritu ad Templum propellebar. Malo spiritu*—the evil wind which, as Baillet later insists, is forcing Descartes "into a place he had voluntarily planned to go," namely, to church.

The next part of the first dream has engendered speculation ranging from the erudite to the hilarious. The Monsieur N. who appears in his dream is probably the dream's abbreviation for Marin Mersenne, Descartes's friend and mentor, eight years his senior and the teacher associated with the happy days at La Flèche. The melon from a foreign land is first a repetition in assonance of M.N. Its meaning is obscure;[14] yet we can try to make sense of it here. The dream ends, and the waking Descartes, who is analyzing his own dreams, decides that an "evil genius" (echoing *malo spiritu*) has tried to seduce him. It is a seduction of intellectual pride, so the deferential Baillet says, firmly guiding us in our own interpretation. Such a reading makes some sense if we remember that Descartes confesses that the day of November 10, spent as it was in mental exaltation, was without any mention or

14. Scharfstein, in "Descartes' Dreams," pp. 304–5, sheds some interesting light on the melon problem, suggesting that its appearance in the dream is stimulated by Saint-Amant's poem "Le melon," coupled with another called "Ode à la solitude." This information seems to me to be helpful in suggesting what the day residue might have been for this dream image. Scharfstein also notes a possible connection between the melon and Descartes's passion for anatomy (and dissection). I would add that the melon also suggests the dissection of the human eye, which Descartes frequently undertook in his study of optics. Such an association will take on greater significance in the section on Freud in this chapter. Gregor Sebba is equally industrious with this mystery, discovering that a fellow student of Descartes's at La Flèche was important enough to be mentioned in a 1641 letter of Descartes's. This student, a certain Chaveau, was from the town of Melun. "A memory arose," writes Sebba, "and was quickly defused by a verbal pun: *Melun* becomes *melon.* Freud would have loved that." Except that he didn't. Sebba, *The Dream of Descartes,* ed. Richard A. Watson (Carbondale and Edwardsville, 1987), p. 14. It has also been suggested to me that melon suggests melancholy. My only comment is that the pun works far better in English than in French and not at all in Latin. Interestingly, Descartes's melon does not appear in the definitive (and likely sole) study of literary melons. See Rolf Norrmann and Jon Haarberb, *Nature and Language: A Semiotic Study of Cucurbits in Literature* (London, 1980).

thought of God. (The second dream will in fact make explicit what the first dream fears but represses: the wrath of God at this intellectual pride.) Whereas the day is described as one of great joy, with Descartes's brain "on fire," the first dream is ushered in by exhaustion and burnout, and marks the place of a *tristis casus*, as the "Olympica" phrased it.

But to return to the melon: Baillet will later tell us that the melon signifies the "charms of solitude" for Descartes, charms "available through purely human attractions"—a reading that is bizarre at best (not to mention unsubtle in its attempt to be oblique), whether it be Descartes's or Baillet's. Adding my voice to the chorus of interpretations (only two of which I have mentioned), I would suggest that the melon (an exotic, rare fruit in seventeenth-century France) represents a displacement of the forbidden fruit of knowledge—the fruit which, as indicated in Descartes's night dreams, has been arrogantly plucked in the day's exalted reverie. The dream shows the fear that there has been a transgression of the divine order; much has been learned that is perhaps not man's to know. The result of eating from the Tree of Knowledge is separation (from Eden, from innocence, from unity of mind and body). The great discovery revealed by the dreams initially announces itself as a *tota simul*, a fundamental unity, but it is the discovery of a unity that necessitates first and foremost a split, a separation, an inability of the mind to walk in step with its own body, a loss of innocence in the movement of the limbs in response to the commands of the brain. This path of life, highlighted by the third dream and problematized by the first, branches out in several directions: backward (past) and forward (future), left and right, back and forth, and around in circles. We do not yet know as we read the first dream that left and right signify science versus philosophy, which will combine into the *mathesis universalis*. The first dream is the dream of separation, of eating the forbidden fruit (Descartes even turns over to his right side after this dream, praying to be saved from his sins).

Later, after the *tota simul* and *mathesis universalis* are harmonized into the *mirabilis scientia*, the foundation of a miraculous science, the same image of transgression (the forbidden fruit) will become a happier metaphor: Descartes's own Tree of Knowledge.

This tree will demonstrate the necessity of separation and division as the grounding for unity. As Descartes draws it, the roots of this tree are metaphysics; the trunk is physics; the three main branches are mechanics, medicine, and morals—the application of knowledge to the external world. Thus the continuity of metaphysics and science, in spite of their apparent split, is the secret to be revealed in the progression of the three dreams. It should be remembered here that this secret is discovered in the same way that philosophy, as Freud notes, finds it great truths—by intuition. Moreover, the intuition comes in the form of a dream. Just as it did, of course, to Freud. The ultimate harmony Descartes finds in the separation of philosophy and science is not only one that Freud never finds but is something that remains a source of ambivalence and conflict throughout his life. But we will return to that problem later.[15]

Descartes's discovery, that division is necessary as the grounding for an ultimate unity, occurs on the Eve of Saint Martin. Baillet reminds us that this is a day of debauchery but hastily assures us that Descartes was not drunk when he had his three dreams. Saint Martin, however, does not merely provide an excuse for reveling; he is the patron saint of the poor and is famous for having once torn his coat in two in order to give one half of it to a pauper. Saint Martin's Day is celebrated even now in many parts of Europe by a figure riding on horseback, playing the role of the saint with his cape torn in two, one half resting on his shoulder. The cape unites the saint with the poor man in a brotherhood of charity.

Is it possible that Descartes unconsciously identifies with the saint of the divided coat? Or with the actor who plays the saint, displaying his emblem in the form of half a cloak? Descartes, it will be remembered, believed he had inherited his pallor and ill health from his mother—a mask of a kind. In January of the same year as the dreams, Descartes writes that he sees himself as playing a part: "As an actor puts on a mask in order that the color

15. For more recent literature on the important connection between Descartes's scientific thought and his philosophy, see *Descartes: Philosophy, Mathematics and Physics*, ed. Stephen Gaukroger, Harvester Readings in the History of Science and Philosophy 1 (Totowa, NJ, 1980).

of his visage may not be seen, so I, who am about to mount upon
the stage of the world of which I have as yet been a spectator
only, appear masked upon the scene."[16] The actor who plays
Saint Martin, his cloak torn in half, is as if symbolic of division,
the second step of the *méthode:* "to divide each problem I examined into as many parts as feasible, and as was requisite for its
better solution."[17]

Francis Barker has convincingly argued a sociohistorical approach to the Cartesian notion of division. He links it to the moment when the ego "Divides itself from itself to become both the
subject and the object of its fabular narration." The bourgeois individual is thus seen as "a split narration isolated within a cen-
sored discourse." I would prefer the word "subject" to "ego" in
this context, but Barker's reading reinforces the resonances of division for Descartes: from the personal they become epistemological and, ultimately, political. The divisive aspects of censorship
are, as we shall see, crucial to my reading of Descartes's own
dilemma.[18]

The second dream takes place after two hours of meditation
and consists in a clap of thunder followed by sparks. Initially, Descartes takes this to be the common manifestation of God (for the
sin of intellectual pride: not only had Descartes failed to mention
God during the whole of November 10, but he had also spent the
day believing he had penetrated the heart of science). Baillet tells
us that Descartes later decided that the thunder (and lightning)
was the spirit of truth, descending upon him in order to possess
him. In any case, this minidream, which begins by instilling terror, ends in relative calm, thus perhaps mirroring the two interpretations just mentioned: the wrath of God followed by the
spirit of truth. The absolute reality of God is conceived of as

16. This famous passage is taken from Descartes's private notes or *Pensées.* The
translation here is adopted from Feuer's "The Dreams of Descartes," p. 26. For the
Latin original, see *Oeuvres de Descartes,* 10:213.

17. Descartes, *Discourse,* in *Philosophical Writings,* p. 20 ("de diviser chacune des
difficultés que j'examinerais en autant de parcelles qu'il se pourrait et qu'il serait
requis pour les mieux résoudre"; *Oeuvres et lettres,* p. 138).

18. Francis Barker, *The Tremulous Body: Essays on Subjection* (New York, 1984),
pp. 55, 57.

simple and spontaneous fact, like lightning, like truth. Truth is established here in relation to the eye, or vision.

Seeing, illumination, sparks, light—all these terms are here essentially identical, having to do with truth. Seeing sparks in the room, Baillet says, was nothing new for Descartes. "But this time he desired philosophical reasons." One can assume that Descartes previously sought scientific explanations for this phenomenon—his work on optics was already well underway at this time. But the day of intense thought, coupled with the context of the first dream and the terror of the second, understandably puts Descartes into a metaphysical (and psychological) rather than an experimental frame of mind.

It is the third dream that is the most famous and the most frequently cited. Descartes first finds a dictionary and then a collection of poetry. He himself offers this analysis: the dictionary is a science, and the book of poetry is "Philosophy and Wisdom joined together." The book contains two poems by Ausonius: the first is "Est et Non" (the yes and no of Pythagoras, as Baillet tells us, and the "Truth and Falsehood in human knowledge and the secular sciences"). Now the thunderclap as spirit of truth becomes that which ushers in the "treasures of all the sciences," so there is a return of sorts to the intellectual arrogance that the thunder seemed initially to chastise.

The second of Ausonius's poems is "Quod vitae sectabor iter?" ("What path of life shall I pursue?"). Here is a poem suggesting the problem of freedom and necessity, but also echoing the question of the first dream: should Descartes continue his life of carefree pleasure, or must he devote himself to God and mind? What path of life to pursue, and how to walk upon it? While the first poem raises the question of science and existence, this second poem raises the question of the *cogito,* the answer to which will eventually be: I will always necessarily choose God.

There are many other wonderful aspects to this dream, including the fact that the books, in good dreamlike fashion, keep appearing and disappearing. But for the present concerns, three things should be noted. First, Descartes loses both poems when he is leafing through another book. This book contains "several

small portraits engraved in copperplate," leading Descartes to declare that the "book was very beautiful, but that it was not of the
same printing as the one [he] had known." So the second thing
to be noted is that this book is not the same as the first, but it is
beautifully illustrated with portraits of copperplate.

The third point is the character of the poet in question, Ausonius. A Latin poet of the fourth century and the governor of Gaul,
Ausonius converted to Christianity for the sake of convenience;
it made his life easier. To turn to Christianity for the sake of convenience is not unrelated to the unspoken problem of the
dreams: the search for the truth at any cost versus the very real
and severe power and rules of the Church. Descartes elects to
pursue the straight and narrow path—in other words, the path
which adheres to the Church's views. The famous 1910 edition
of the *Encyclopaedia Britannica* put it rather neatly: "Descartes was
not disposed to be a martyr; he had a sincere respect for the
church, and had no wish to begin an open conflict with established doctrines."[19] The first dream is generally read to be about
Descartes's relation to the past; the second, as the spontaneous—
alethic—presence of God; and the third, as the contemplation of
Descartes's future course in life. All this is clear enough. But I
want to argue that this last dream is even more about the future
than first appears. The last dream prefigures, and even puts into
place, what we may call the recantation Descartes will set into
motion after he learns what happened to Galileo.

The third dream is the one in which Descartes chooses what
path of life to follow; it is a path already marked out by Ausonius.
The half-sleeping Descartes will interpret the "Quod vitae" poem
to "mark the sound advice of a wise person, or even of Moral
Theology." And yet it is Ausonius who will have already cut out
the path that Descartes will take fourteen years later when he
shelves *Le Monde,* his work on cosmology, because he has learned
of Galileo's fate at the hands of the Church authorities. Like Galileo, Descartes had intended to adhere to a Copernican notion of
the universe. But in 1633, near the end of that year, Descartes
writes to Mersenne that *Le Monde* will not be sent to him: "I had

19. *Encyclopaedia Britannica,* 11th ed., s.v. "Descartes."

intended sending you my *World* . . . but I have just been at Leyden and Amsterdam to ask after Galileo's cosmical system as I imagined I had heard of its being printed last year in Italy. I was told that it had been printed, but that every copy had been at the same time burnt at Rome, and that Galileo had been himself condemned to some penalty."[20] Is, then, the evil wind that throws Descartes against the church door—where he wanted to go anyway, he complains—none other than Descartes himself, whose mind is at odds with his faith, and whose politics are in collision with his discovery? Is Descartes walking out of step with himself?

I am not chastising Descartes for cowardice: no good would have been served had his *Monde* received the same fate as Galileo's work. And to be fair to Descartes, it should also be said that he was as worried about truncating his work on cosmology as he was about getting into trouble with the Church: "But, since for nothing in the world would I wish to produce a discourse in which the Church could find a single word with which to disagree, I prefer to suppress it, rather than to have it appear in crippled form."[21] Moreover, a few months later Descartes began to feel that someday the "world" would be ready for his.

Nevertheless, it should be remembered that the first moral law drawn from the *Méthode* (in the third part of the *Discourse*) is obedience: "to obey the laws and customs of my country; faithfully keeping to the religion in which by God's favour I was brought up from childhood."[22] But even if we give Descartes the most

20. Ibid. ("je m'étais proposé de vous envoyer mon *Monde* . . . mais m'étant fait enquérir ces jours à Leyde et à Amsterdam si le *Système du Monde* de Galilée n'y était point, à cause qu'il me semblait avoir appris qu'il avait été imprimé en Italie l'anneé passée, on m'a mandé qu'il était vrai qu'il avait été imprimé, mais que tous les exemplaires en avaient été brulés à Rome au même temps, et lui condamné à quelque amende"; Descartes to Mersenne, November 1633, *Oeuvres et lettres*, p. 947).

21. "Mais comme je ne voudrais pour rien du monde qu'il sortît de moi un discours, où il se trouvât le moindre mot qui fût désapprouvé de l'Eglise, aussi aime-je mieux le supprimer, que de le faire paraître estropié." Ibid., p. 948; my translation. There is an interesting confusion here between le *Monde* and le monde, which reminds us of the political and cosmological dyad which for Descartes constitute the notion "world."

22. "d'obéir aux lois et aux coûtumes de mon pays, retenant constamment la religion en laquelle Dieu m'a fait la grâce d'être instruit dès mon enfance." Ibid., p. 14; translated in *Discourse*, in *Philosophical Writings*, p. 24.

generous reading, the presence of Ausonius in this text is not coincidental; Ausonius too, chooses to "obey the laws and customs" of his country. Significant too is the way the third dream chooses to resolve the question of what path is to be taken in the light of Descartes's dangerous views. And then there is the obscure matter of the odd copperplates. We should be alerted to their importance by the way in which the text tries to dismiss them: "There was left for him only to explain the little portraits in copper-plate, which he had found in the second book."

Baillet tells us that Descartes stopped looking for an explanation when "an Italian painter visited him the next day." Such a statement makes no sense at all, even on the most superficial level, unless we remember that, in Descartes's day, dreams were considered to be prophetic at times—and prophetic, often, of banal events. I think that when the Italian painter came to visit, Descartes conveniently decided that that part of the dream simply foresaw the event, for copperplates were best executed in Italy by Italian artists.

For Descartes, Italy is above all the land of Galileo, already in trouble for his views at the time of the dreams. In this last dream, the copperplates appear in a book which is beautiful but "not of the same printing as the one he had known." The piece "Est et Non" is missing, and the dictionary is "not complete as it had been when he saw it the first time." The dream, then, is about censorship and recantation. It is about a book which is lost and found again, but altered—an alteration even the pretty copperplates cannot mask. So another split can be discerned: the stranger who disappears with the books is like the part of Descartes that wants to have the "original" work, the one he remembers. And then there is the Descartes who holds in his hands the revised book, with the plates.

Is Galileo sending a message to Descartes in the form of a melon (itself reminiscent of a cosmos, a world)?[23] Galileo's work, of course, was also in optics, a field shared by Descartes. The cutting of lenses is not unrelated to the cutting of copperplates; simi-

23. Descartes's friend and teacher Mersenne (Monsieur N. in the dream?) was in communication with Galileo as early as 1610. Mersenne himself was viewed as a link between philosophers and scientists in Europe, the two realms of knowl-

lar tools and techniques are used. Moreover, it is with copperplates that Descartes himself was to illustrate his work on
optics, begun in Paris in 1613 when Descartes met Claude My-
dorge, the great lens maker. And optics for Descartes is also tied
to the "Est et Non"; it is by opening and closing his eyes (as in
the second dream, and as at the end of the third) that Descartes
ascertains whether something exists or not, whether it is true or
false, imagined or real. The eye is both a physical mechanism to
be explained and, metaphorically (as represented by the mind),
the primary organ of knowledge for Descartes. So too with Galileo, for whom his telescope was to prove his cosmology. The violent censorship visited upon Galileo will become a self-imposed
censorship in Descartes.

Such censorship is mirrored in Baillet himself. The first biography was published in 1691 in two volumes and contains the texts
of the three dreams. Baillet was a priest who prided himself on
working all but five hours out of every twenty-four. He was not
pleased when in 1692 a vicious attack on his biography of Descartes appeared. Entitled *Réflexions d'un académicien sur la vie de M.
Descartes envoyées à un de ses amis en Hollande,* the work was anonymous but generally attributed to Gilles Ménage, the famous literary critic. It consists of two "letters" from Paris, one dated November 15, 1691, and the other November 22. These letters attack
Baillet on every level: his knowledge of classical works, contemporary works, history, historical method, logic, and so on. They
also attack Baillet's conclusion to the dream sequence. Out of
context, Baillet appears foolish (as he sometimes does in context),
and Descartes, drunk.

Baillet's answer to the *Réflexions* was the greatly abridged 1693
edition of the biography, in which the dream sequence disappears
altogether, replaced by a paragraph summarizing the importance
of the dreams.[24] Since the original document, "Olympica," is now
inaccessible as well, Baillet's skill as an interpreter appears con-

---

edge which the dreams try to fuse. Mersenne's gift is in a sense this link—a Galileo—to which Descartes will add philosophy. See, too, Feuer's reading, which
raises many of the same points and reaches entirely different conclusions. "The
Dreams of Descartes," p. 22.

24. I discovered this well-known act of censorship (or "editing") for myself
when I used the 1693 edition in the University of Chicago library. After much

veniently unimpeachable. In the introduction to the 1693 (abridged) text, Baillet says that this new edition represents the original of 1691 "as a miniature represents a portrait" (*comme une miniature represente un portrait*). Just as the copperplate portraits in the third dream marked the place of censorship, here Baillet actually labels his own censorship a "portrait." In any case, the two later editions, considerably smaller than the two-volume first one, are cheaper as well, suggesting the great popularity of Baillet's work in, as he would have wished it, abridged form. (Indeed, the abridgment was reprinted as late as the 1950s.)

So the father of modern philosophy, as Descartes is called, has three dreams, which in turn father his thought. These dreams are expunged from the "official" biography by the obsequious Baillet, who, it should be noted, once got into trouble himself with the Church authorities for his *Saints' Lives*. It seems that Baillet was skeptical of the miracles attributed to his subjects. With Descartes, however, Baillet was more than willing to believe the miracle of the dreams, and even to rhapsodize in his interpretation of them. But when Baillet is attacked in the *Réflexions,* the dreams, and their context, promptly vanish. In this text, then, we have a triad structure, not only of the dreams but of the three censors or recanters as well—Ausonius, Descartes, and Baillet.

But there is, of course, a fourth: Freud will enter this hierarchy by inscribing his own censorship of the dreams. To contextualize such censorship, let us pause to remember that Descartes is the philosopher who declares awareness to be one and the same as the mind: "By the term thinking (*cogitationis*), I mean everything that takes place inside ourselves so that we are aware of it."[25] The notion that all mental activity is conscious stands diametrically opposed, needless to say, to one of the major tenets of psychoanalysis: that there is an Other inside the Subject itself, unreach-

---

rereading, I began to suspect that the dreams had mysteriously disappeared from the biography, much like Emma Bovary from her own novel in Woody Allen's story "The Kugelmass Episode." Thus this censorship in itself is a moment in which Baillet mirrors the third dream.

25. "Par le mot de penser, j'entends tout ce qui se fait en nous de telle sorte que nous l'apercevons immédiatement par nous-mêmes." *Oeuvres et lettres,* p. 574; my translation. Anscombe and Geach translate *penser* (thinking) as "conscious experience," which is a good way of insisting upon Descartes's point of equating consciousness with any form of awareness.

able and largely unknowable, and that this Other is the unconscious. For Descartes, as Hegel remarks, "being and thought are in themselves the same." [26]

Before we dismiss Cartesianism altogether from psychoanalysis, we should note that Descartes's famous dualism—the split between body and mind—is a bipartite structure appropriated by psychoanalysis as the dialectical construct of conscious and unconscious, subject and other, eros and the death instinct ("Thanatos," as it is pretentiously called in the English translation). Moreover, as we have already noted, the inherent unity in all things which Descartes presents rests first in division, both in the initial steps of the *Méthode* and in the famous body/mind cleavage: *una est in rebus,* the *tota simul,* and the *mathesis universalis,* are grounded in duality and division. The transparency between being and thought to which Hegel points in Descartes is possible only by division, by complete enumeration, and by the implied *ergo* which acts as the pivot between the *cogito* and *sum.* Hence Poulet's notion that there is in Descartes a doubling of the subject (or of being), a split of the subject from itself, even if there is a transparency between consciousness and mind. We are not so far from psychoanalysis after all.

For Descartes, the mind is fundamentally indivisible, and it should apply itself to that which it can know: "We must," he writes, "occupy ourselves only with those objects that our intellectual powers appear competent to know certainly and indubitably." [27] Surely here we have found a principle that goes against everything Freud believes in, for his psychoanalysis concentrates itself on the unconscious—precisely that which remains uncertain and doubtful as an object of knowledge for the mind. Yet Freud's response to Descartes's dreams seems to adhere to Des-

26. G. W. F. Hegel, *Phenomenology of Spirit,* trans. A. V. Miller (Oxford, 1977), pp. 351–52.

27. *Rules for the Direction of the Mind,* in *Philosophical Writings,* p. 153 ("Il ne faut s'occuper que des objets dont notre esprit paraît capable d'acquérir une connaissance certaine et indubitable"; *Oeuvres et lettres,* p. 39). One of Kant's many debts to Descartes is evident here, especially with regard to the first *Kritik* and its scorn for speculative metaphysics. For the more usual view of the cogito, see Jean-Luc Marion, *Questions cartésiennes: Méthode et métaphysique* (Paris, 1991). See too his reading of the three dreams, pp. 7–36. For Marion, the dreams awaken the *Cogitatio.*

cartes's principles rather than to his own. Freud will claim he cannot concern himself with dreams that can remain uncertain to him. One can accuse Freud here of a certain epistemologically oriented imitative fallacy.

In 1929, Freud was asked by Maxime Leroy to take a look at Descartes's dreams. Leroy was working on his book *Descartes, le philosophe au masque*. As usual, Freud did his homework. Although Leroy paraphrased Baillet's own paraphrasing of the dreams (and Leroy's summary is inaccurate and bizarre), Freud took the time to study Baillet's full text.[28] In his response to Leroy, Freud stresses that he first felt dismay, since he could not ask Descartes himself to free-associate. But then the task "turned out to be easier than I anticipated." He adds cautiously, however, "The fruit of my investigations will no doubt seem to you much less important than you had a right to expect" (SD, p. 203). This is typical of Freud's opening remarks, which are nearly always apologetic and modest; but one wonders here whether he is blaming the paucity of his own remarks on the dreams themselves or on some inadequacy in himself. By what right, in other words, did Leroy have reason to expect more from Freud?

Freud first says that these dreams are "dreams from above" (*Träume von oben*). This assertion is remarkable because it is identical to the one used by Baillet to describe the dreams: as Baillet leads into the dreams, he tells us that Descartes believed they could only have come "from above"—"Il s'imagina ne pouvoir etre venus d'enhaut."[29] But whereas Descartes means that the dreams were from heaven (and not, as yet another attack on Baillet suggested, two years after the first edition, "ordinary dreams aroused by tobacco, beer, and melancholy"),[30] Freud means the opposite. Dreams from above, he says, "are formulations of ideas which could have been created just as well in a waking state as

28. Strachey points this out in his note to Freud's response to Leroy. Freud must have consulted Baillet, because while Leroy mentions only a "melon," it is Baillet who says that it comes from "a foreign land," the terms by which Freud refers to it. "Some Dreams of Descartes': A Letter to Maxime Leroy," *Standard Edition*, 21:199–204; further references to this letter will be abbreviated SD.

29. Baillet, *La Vie de Monsieur Descartes*, 1:81.

30. See *Nouveaux mémoire pour servir à l'histoire du cartésianisme par M.G. de l'A.* (1692), pp. 43–44. Adam and Tannery note that the author is Gilles de l'Aunay, that is, Pierre-Daniel Huet, bishop of Avranches; see *Oeuvres de Descartes*, 10:185.

during the state of sleep, and which have derived their content only in certain parts from mental states at a comparatively deep level. That is why these dreams offer for the most part a content which has an abstract, poetic or symbolic form" (SD, p. 203).

In 1923, six years earlier, Freud had also written on dreams from above. They correspond, he wrote then, to "thoughts or intentions of the day before which have contrived during the night to obtain reinforcement from repressed material that is debarred from the ego. When this is so, analysis as a rule disregards this unconscious ally and succeeds in inserting the latent dreamthoughts into the texture of waking thought." [31] It should be noted, among other things, that the unconscious portion of "dreams from above" is "disregarded" by analysis. In any case, this definition is surely meant, from Freud's point of view, to serve as a viable description of Descartes and the production of his dreams, especially in relation to the day of ecstasy that preceded them.

The dream from above is from a deep level of the mind, but accessible because it could have been created "just as well" when the subject was awake. "We cannot understand the dream," Freud continues in his response to Leroy, "but the dreamer—or patient—can translate it immediately and without difficulty, given that the content of the dream is very close to his conscious thoughts. There then remain certain parts . . . which belong to the unconscious and which are in many respects the most interesting" (SD, p. 203). It is significant that Freud begins, in the same terms as Baillet, by proclaiming Descartes's dreams to be essentially *conscious:* the dreams of the philosopher of consciousness, in other words, match his waking thought.

The "above" here is not heaven, of course ("This term must be understood in a psychological, not in a mystical, sense," says Freud of the "dreams from above"), but rather the outside, conscious, waking world. Freud's topographic model of the mind recapitulates this understanding of "above" (north, so to speak) and "below." We have already noted, however, that such an up/

---

31. Freud, "Remarks on the Theory and Practice of Dream-Interpretation as a Whole," *Standard Edition,* 19:111.

down and inside/outside topography is not innocent; it belies a protoromantic notion of inspiration, and thus of creativity. The question here is, Whose "inside" is being privileged? Whose "above" being dismissed? "This way of judging 'dreams from above,'" Freud continues to Leroy, "is the one to be followed in the case of Descartes' dreams" (SD, p. 203). The insistence on the same terminology as Baillet is acknowledged, for Freud uses the same phrase with an inverted sense: a dream from above has come, with psychoanalysis, from consciousness. If the "below," as Jean Starobinski has shown, is modeled on the hell of the ancients—the Infernal Regions, to use Virgil's term—it is also the place of the profound, of what is worth taking note of.[32] Freud, in reading Descartes's dreams, attempts (and achieves) an inversion of the map of values: heaven (north) is of little interest; but hell is teeming with meaning and significance. The implication, then, is that Descartes, like his dreams, is shallow, as is any philosophy which privileges consciousness.

But as all dreams for Freud must have some element of the unconscious, there will be parts, he reminds us, even in a dream from "above," which will remain inexplicable; and those parts are from "below," from the unconscious. It will come as no surprise that the "parts" of Descartes's dreams which Freud finds inexplicable, and therefore from the unconscious, are the melon and the copperplate portraits. In the final four short paragraphs of his reading, Freud makes four main points: (1) We should accept Descartes's own interpretation of the dreams, but we ourselves (using Descartes's own metaphor) "have no path open to us which will take us any further." (2) The hindrances that prevent Descartes from moving in the first dream are "an internal conflict," the left side representing evil and sin, and the wind an evil genius. (3) Descartes would have known all of the figures in the dream, but we cannot. (4) The melon is certainly not a symbol for the "charms of solitude," but Descartes could probably have shed some light on it. "If it is correlated with his state of sin," Freud goes on to say, "this association might stand for a sexual

---

32. See Starobinski's "*Acheronta Movebo,*" in Meltzer, *The Trial(s) of Psychoanalysis,* pp. 273–86. Starobinski makes the most compelling analysis I have seen for Freud's debt to Virgil.

picture which occupied the lonely young man's imagination." The final sentence to Leroy reads, "On the question of the portraits Descartes throws no light" (SD, p. 204).

Freud has spent a mere one and a half pages discussing the most famous dreams in philosophy. And while his lack of interest in them may be relegated to his proclaimed distaste for philosophy in general, to his terribly busy schedule, or to the fact that he admittedly could not put Descartes on the couch, I think we must be suspicious of the whole business. If we take Freud's own texts to read these same dreams that Freud tells us are unreadable, we fare much better. In part, of course, we have already been doing this. My reading of the dreams—the suggestions concerning Ausonius, Galileo, Mersenne, and so on—impose Freud's own dream interpretation theory upon the dream texts of Descartes. Moreover, Descartes himself analyzes his dreams, and Freud says that he does a credible job: "The philosopher interprets them himself and, in accordance with all the rules for the interpretation of dreams, we must accept his interpretation, but it should be added that we have no path open to us which will take us any further" (SD, p. 204). Yet Freud's own dream interpretation allows us to go farther still.

It will be recalled that Freud cannot, and will not, make anything of the melon or the little portraits. He seems befuddled by them. And yet in the second chapter of his dream book, in the section on the specimen dream, Freud says: "There is at least one spot in every dream at which it is unplumbable—a navel, as it were, that is its point of contact with the unknown" (*ID*, p. 111 n. 1). In the seventh chapter he again refers to "the dream's navel, the spot where it reaches down into the unknown" (*ID*, p. 525). We are back to "above" and "below" terminology: every dream, even one from "above," has something in it from "below," and that is the navel. We could just leave it at that, and call the melon and the portraits the blind spots in Descartes's dreams. But we have already gone a bit farther than that with both. In any case, the blind spot is the dream's own censorship—from "below."

Freud quickly drops the discussion of the little portraits. But we can consider the fact, for example, that Baillet's French version refers to the portraits as being *de taille douce*. *Tailler* is a verb used, among other things, to describe the cutting of glass, and it is used frequently by Baillet in this context.[33] We have already noted that Descartes worked on optics in Paris as early as 1613. He drew elaborate charts of the eye, of perspective, and of refraction. He worked on lenses (as did Galileo). There would be a natural association here for Freud, one which he passes over: in the botanical monograph dream, the first fully discussed dream in *The Interpretation of Dreams*, a book lies before Freud, and he is turning over a folded colored plate. Bound in each copy is a dried specimen of the plant, "as though it had been taken from a herbarium" (*ID*, p. 169). The botanical monograph dream is strangely like the third dream of Descartes: a book lies before the dreamer, and it contains a plate that illustrates the contents. The dream suggests an entire method of thought (much as Descartes's dreams imitate the heuristic moves of his own *méthode*). More importantly, however, Freud associates the plant with the coca plant, the subject of one of his monographs, which, like Descartes's work, was illustrated by his own hand.

That monograph had to do with the uses and properties of cocaine. But at the crucial moment in his research, in 1884, Freud had gone to Hamburg to see his fiancée. It is she who was later blamed when, during Freud's absence, his friend Karl Koller rubbed some cocaine in the eye of a dog and "discovered" an ophthalmic anesthesia.[34] This discovery brought Koller instant fame. Because he did not have publication priority, Freud's studious monograph "Über Koka," from the same year, fell into oblivion. (This was Martha's fault, as we have seen—a conclusion which heralds the assumptions in *Civilization and Its Discontents* concerning women and how they obstruct the creative work of

33. For Marion, Descartes will correctly interpret the little portraits (in *spite* of the Italian anecdote) later, in the *Diotropique* (1637) as a form of what Marion calls de-figuration. *Questions cartésiennes*, p. 27, n. 22.

34. Ernest Jones dubs this incident Freud's second chance at a fame which eluded him, the first having been the use of gold chloride to stain nervous tissue. See Jones, *The Life and Work of Sigmund Freud*, 3 vols. (New York, 1953–57), 1:78–79.

men.)[35] The claim to originality, and its concomitant fame, had eluded him because he didn't get there first.

Now here is another monograph entitled *The Interpretation of Dreams*, the basis of which is Freud's own dreams, dreams that demonstrate the method. Freud describes the dreams and then interprets them—just as Descartes did. The botanical monograph dream with the dream of Irma's injection are specimen dreams marking out this method, echoing Descartes.

When Freud sets about analyzing his botanical monograph dream, he associates rather quickly to the coca plant and his lost chance at certain fame: "I had myself indicated this application [Koller's discovery of cocaine as an anesthetic] but I had not been thorough enough to pursue the matter further" (*ID*, p. 170). From there he lapses into "a kind of daydream." If he should ever get glaucoma, he muses, there would be a possible collegial awkwardness when Dr. Freud became the patient Freud. He would keep his identity a secret, he decides: "The operating surgeon, who would have no idea of my identity, would boast once again of how easily such operations could be performed since the introduction of cocaine; and I should not give the slightest hint that I myself had had a share in the discovery" (*ID*, p. 170). There is a curious rhetoric here: Freud wants to keep "secret" his identity, something few people would care to know about at this point in his career (especially with respect to cocaine research), since fame has thus far eluded him. Then Freud suddenly remembers, at the end of his daydream, that his father "had in fact been attacked by glaucoma." During the operation, Freud's friend Dr.

---

35. The argument about how women obstruct the work of geniuses is made by Nietzsche: "The danger for artists, for geniuses . . . is woman: adoring women confront them with corruption. Hardly any of them have character enough not to be corrupted—or 'redeemed'—when they find themselves treated like gods: soon they condescend to the level of the women." *The Case of Wagner,* in *The Birth of Tragedy and the Case of Wagner,* trans. Walter Kaufmann (New York, 1967), p. 161. I cite this passage, not because (to put it mildly) it is an unusual view, but rather because of the particular peerage in which it puts Freud, who maintained that he never read philosophy and particularly avoided "the very great pleasure of reading the work of Nietzsche." This unknown pleasure can only be "very great," if we believe Freud when he says that he hasn't read the German philosopher, because he knows that there is a rather striking kinship of ideas. And if he has read him (which is far more likely), mutatis mutandis.

Leopold Königstein had been the surgeon and Koller himself was in charge of the cocaine anesthesia. The latter had commented that "this case brought together all of the three men who had had a share in the introduction of cocaine" (*ID*, p. 171).

Koller's egalitarian view generously puts all three scientists—himself, Königstein, and Freud—into the same position of importance with respect to the use of cocaine in ophthalmic surgery. In fact, however, what emerges is Freud's frustration at not having been recognized more fully for his personal share in the "discovery" (the same word, as we have noted, which Freud used to describe his work in psychoanalysis). We could say, a bit unkindly, that Freud didn't want to share in the "discovery" at all: he wanted to be the first, and the only one recognized in his research.

The botanical monograph dream is the dream of a rivalry with a peer over optics: "Once, I recalled, I really *had* written something in the nature of a *monograph on a plant*, namely a dissertation on the coca-plant (Freud, 1884), which had drawn Karl Koller's attention to the anesthetic properties of cocaine" (*ID*, p. 170). Freud, in other words, considers himself to have been the inspiration for the idea later attributed to Koller. As far as Freud is concerned, intellectually he *did* have priority; what he failed to get, and wants, is public recognition. The rivalry Freud feels between himself and Koller mirrors the Descartes dreams at two levels: first, by the implied other rivalry between Descartes and Galileo (with Mersenne and his melon serving as mediator); and, second, by a rivalry Freud himself may well feel with Descartes, whose "Olympica" founded "modern philosophy" with no questions asked about originality. *The Interpretation of Dreams* is meant to be the monograph that succeeds where "Über Koka" failed. But Descartes had succeeded the first time.

There is a third mirroring here, too, one of which Freud was unaware: Descartes's increasing fear that his work was being "stolen"—in particular, as mentioned earlier, by his friend Beeckman. In 1630, Descartes accuses Beeckman of plagiarizing from his *Treatise on Music.* Moreover, Descartes's obsessive worries about his claims to originality and attribution may have been justified, since it is frequently remarked that the *méthode* was not invented by him at all, but by Pierre de la Ramée.

Freud's own obsession with originality and fame has been thoroughly documented, as has his concern with having his ideas stolen.[36] This obsession may explain why Descartes's copperplates, so resonant in sound and significance to Freud's colored plates, should remain a mystery for Freud; and this mystery, coupled with the subsequent indifference on Freud's part to the dreams of the French philosopher, is the first clue that something is afoot. The reader of Freud jumps to associate Descartes's text to Freud's. Only Freud remains in the dark and can, in his words, "throw no light" on the matter.

The first Descartes dream is also open to a Freudian interpretation, which the founder of psychoanalysis bypasses. Indeed, it might be seen as a "typical" dream, in the group called "embarrassing dreams of being naked" in the fifth chapter of the dream book. Dreams of being naked are dreams of exhibition, Freud tells us there. Baillet, let us note, says that throughout the day of November 10, Descartes rendered his mind naked: *Son imagination lui presentat son esprit tout nud.* Such dreams, Freud goes on to explain, are associated with difficulty in walking: "one *does* feel

36. See, e.g., Paul Roazen's *Brother Animal: The Story of Freud and Tausk* (New York, 1969), which documents the complexities of the Freud, Tausk, and Lou Andreas-Salomé triangle of competition. For the second triangle of rivalry—Freud, Tausk, and Deutsch—see Neil Hertz, "Freud and the Sandman," in *Textual Strategies: Perspectives in Post-Structuralist Criticism,* ed. Josue V. Harari (Ithaca, NY, 1979), pp. 296–321. Finally, for an argument that Freud recanted his own findings in order to have his views be more palatable and reach a larger audience, see Jeffrey Moussaieff Masson, *The Assault on the Truth: Freud's suppression of the Seduction Theory* (New York, 1984). Recantation and censorship are related in a manner best articulated through Freud's own terms: the unconscious, for Freud, is discovered only to be lost again (repressed) and then rediscovered. Recantation and censorship both partake of this larger dynamic of repression, which functions politically as well as psychically in this context. In the Descartes-Freud connection, there is repression that we can call psychical (censorship within the dreams; authorial self-censorship in retelling and interpreting them; and recantation, or denial, of what appears to be a frightening discovery). On the political level, there is repression of a discovery through the actual or anticipated censorship by the authorities (the cosmology for Descartes and the seduction theory for Freud) and the possibility that a refusal to recant will result in being exiled, either literally (in Descartes's case, the possibility of excommunication) or textually (remaining unpublished or banned from whatever canon is addressed).

shame and embarrassment and tries to escape or hide, and is then overcome by a strange inhibition which prevents one from moving and makes one feel incapable of altering one's distressing situation" (*ID*, p. 242). Then Freud alludes to a dream of his own in which he suddenly is unable to move (up a flight of stairs). He adds that in dreams of this sort, onlookers rarely notice the dreamer's difficulty, though they themselves have no such problems of locomotion.

Here again, then, Freud might have contributed to the Descartes dream sequence. But there is more: it is in the description of this type of dream that Freud makes the connection between typical dreams and creative writing: "It sometimes happens that the sharp eye of a creative writer has an analytic realization of the process of transformation of which he is habitually no more than the tool. If so, he may follow the process in reverse direction and so trace back the imaginative writing to a dream" (*ID*, p. 246). Does not this last sentence describe *both* Descartes and Freud? Is Freud afraid that his new theory will, unlike Descartes's, prove to be a fraud? Is that why, in this same section on this type of dream, he mentions the fable of the emperor's new clothes? Revealing the nakedness of the mind can sometimes lead to nothing at all, as in the case of the cocaine papers. Worse still, nakedness can reveal that there is nothing there to conceal, no secret worth keeping ("In This House, on July 24th, 1895, the Secret of Dreams was Revealed to Dr. Sigm. Freud"; or "I should not give the slightest hint that I myself had had a share in the discovery"). Fame, after all, engenders a symbiosis between "discovery" and "identity": Freud knows that he has no identity unless he discovers something which will be rightfully attributed to him. The primary text for Descartes's written work is his own dreams; so too for Freud. Descartes dreams his consecutive dreams and ushers in a "new" system of thought (at least, as far as Freud knows); so, Freud hopes, will he. Freud's fear of failure to be original may well explain his dismissal of Descartes's dreams.

There is yet another detail that Freud might have noted—an association, once again, that might have linked the Descartes dreams to Freud's own work. In "The Dream and the Primal

Scene," he tells us that the Wolf-Man suffered from malaria as a young boy, having an attack every day "at a particular hour." This factor, says Freud in a note, is metamorphosed in the patient's dreams while he is in treatment; the malaria will be replaced by a violent wind in the Wolf-Man's dreams.[37] Freud realizes this is a pun for the mal-aria (evil wind). This *ventus malus* is almost identical to the term Descartes used to describe the wind in his first dream: *malo spiritu*. But, as we have pointed out, Descartes's dream puts wind together with spirit, a combination traditional in ancient Greek and Hebrew.

The God-spirit connection is, of course, linked with creation; in Genesis, it is the wind and spirit of God hovering over the waters that begin the moment of creation. (Indeed, in the Descartes dream, the wind pushes him into a place where he had wanted to go, thus plagiarizing his desire.) In the same passage where Hegel discusses Descartes's transparency of being and thought, he distinguishes between two Enlightenments: one calls "being" a predicateless Absolute (spirit or God), and the other calls it matter, or Nature. But, he contends, the distinction is a false one, since unconscious (spirit or God) and conscious (Nature or matter) are in fact the same Notion: "The difference lies not in what they actually are, but simply and solely in the different starting-points of the two developments; and in the fact that each sticks to its own point in the movement of thought."[38]

Perhaps Freud's problem with Descartes is that the French philosopher, echoed differently by Hegel, says that the secret of the *tota simul* is that the mind is one, and that any attempt to distinguish between conscious and unconscious mind impoverishes it. Since Freud believes his greatest discovery to have been the unconscious, his originality (not to mention his system of thought) is in jeopardy if he, in turn, takes the discovery of Descartes seriously: that consciousness and unconsciousness, like spirit or God and the manifestations thereof, are done a disservice, as it were, when they are discussed as separate units. This is part of the secret of Descartes's dreams and is in direct conflict with the philos-

37. Freud, "The Dream and the Primal Scene," *Standard Edition*, 17:37, n. 1.
38. *Phenomenology of Spirit*, pp. 351–52.

ophy Freud builds on the secret of his own dreams. What is ultimately at issue, then, is the very concept of creativity, and what
Hegel calls the mind's "starting point."

The insistence on originality has here replaced the desire for
"Truth" (it is Freud, after all, who says that there is not much
proof that man is even comfortable with the idea of truth), but it
is partly a historical insistence, as I have already shown. Freud's
plant in the botanical monograph dream is also a common post-
organicist symbol for original genius. The plant contains the seed
which, like the genius (no longer evil), already possesses all of the
makings of its mature manifestation. The dream marks Freud's
obsession with originality, and prefigures his later fear that his
ideas will be plagiarized by his associates. Both the obsession and
the fear are symptoms of an unswerving desire for fame and recognition. Fame with dreams, if not with cocaine. These obses-
sions and fears may also be the phantoms of Descartes's dreams;
the French philosopher shared Freud's fears much more than
Freud ever knew. It is Descartes, after all, who refers to the "force
of the imagination" in terms which sound very like the organicists: imagination emits "the seeds of wisdom (which are found
in the minds of all men, like the sparks of fire in flintstones) with
much more ease and brilliance even than Reason can among the
philosophers." Further, "inside" belongs to the romantics no
more than does "originality": Petrarch, for example, warns that
keeping your own thoughts inside you is like asking for others
to pluck them from you, and adds that the "transformation" of
another's idea is to be expected: "Take care that what you have
gathered does not long remain in its original form inside of you:
the bees would not be glorious if they did not convert what they
found into something different and something better" (*Famil-
iarum rerum libri* I.8.23).[39]

---

39. Here I disagree with Thomas Mallon's engaging book, *Stolen Words: Forays
Into the Origins and Ravages of Plagiarism* (New York, 1989). Mallon argues that,
until the seventeenth century, originality as a notion carried no weight, and that
theft was both expected and overlooked. As Mallon himself admits, however, several instances in literature (and more in science) demonstrate that authors have
always been concerned about their intellectual property rights. Or, as Derrida
might put it, originality is an inevitable offshoot of logocentrism, and begins with
the very notion of a beginning.

When Freud writes to Leroy that ultimately the reading of Descartes's dreams "turned out to be easier than I anticipated" (SD, p. 203), he is admitting to an ease that should not by now surprise us, since his own method teaches us that what is *too* evident usually signifies denial. The denial here, as I have argued, is of the possibility that the unconscious, hence Freud's original "discovery," may not exist. It may also be a denial of the suspicion that the concept of "originality" as a single, new, spontaneous event springing alone from an individual mind may be another fantasy. Such a fantasy might, to use Freud's own terms, arise more out of the needs of the ego and superego than out of any noble decision to devote one's life to searching for the truth. For the originality we want to have spring from "inside" us must, if Freud is right, finally tell us more about our notion of the human psyche than about the greatness of any personal achievement. And here Freud is at odds with his own ambition: the founder of psychoanalysis runs into Sigmund Freud. The former could destroy the romantic notion of "genius" in a minute; the latter is not about to give it up.

The reading of Descartes's dreams as being dreams "from above" (echoing Baillet's "d'enhaut"), and as *conscious* dreams born of waking moments, is like an unwilled acquiescence (what I have cumbersomely called an epistemological imitative fallacy) to both Descartes's seamless mind and Baillet's prejudiced reading. There is still, however, the unresolved matter of the melon ("the fruit of [my] investigations," one might say)—that cord leading to the unknown, which Freud hopes he can call the unconscious. The birth imagery of the navel is again connected to Freud's problem with originality, of course. By insisting that every dream has a navel, and thus an unconscious, Freud gives birth, in each dream, to his discovery. The very choice of the term "navel" belies the romantic politics of originality. Thus genius remains *original* but also, therefore, fallible, personal, and imminently vulnerable to the whims of fate (Koller) and the hands of thieves (Tausk, Jung, and others).

It must be noted here that Freud echoes the Frühromantiker as well in his connection of art with sickness. Friedrich Schlegel, Wackenroder, Tieck, Novalis, Eichendorff, to name a few, all call art a *Krankheit,* an illness that is incurable, if noble.[40] For Freud, the need to produce art is frequently the symptom of a neurosis, the assumption being that a successful analysis will "cure" the artist of the need to make art.[41] But sickness here also plays a different, less acknowledged role. Contrary to the psychoanalytic view just mentioned, which wants to see creativity as a neurotic symptom or displacement, the ambition-driven but as yet unknown "genius" is ill until he creates. Descartes, we have seen, lost his pallor, his insomnia, and even his cough after the three dreams which inaugurated the creation of the *méthode.* Freud loses his conviction that he is dying of cancer after he writes *The Interpretation of Dreams.* In both cases, illness (real or imagined, it makes no difference in this situation) is the result of being unable to "create" and thus unable to attain recognition.

In short, it is Freud's method of approaching the dream text that first teaches us to gloss, at least in part, the dreams from which Freud turns away. And this same "method" helps to trace Freud's fear of failure, which in this case results in a blindness to a text—a text that perhaps too easily moves from dream to method, and from there to fame. It is a text, further, that joins literature (the *corpus poetarum*) to science and creates what is acknowledged to be an "original," accepted philosophy. It is a canonized text.

And there is an even more insidious problem: any obsession with recognition entails demonstrating originality; and any such attempt in turn generates the fear of being robbed. As Freud increasingly experiences this fear, the claims to originality become louder. The same holds true for Descartes, so that Freud's view of creativity cannot so easily be tied to the eighteenth-century organicist texts with their insistence on seeing creativity, the way

40. The best example of this in my view, although there are many, is the so-called Berglinger episode in *Herzensergiessungen eines Kunstliebenden Klosterbruders,* traditionally attributed to Wackenroder and Tieck. On questions of attribution, see Martin Bollacher, "Wackenroder und Tieck's Anteile in die *Herzensergiessungen* und *Phantasien,*" in *Wackenroder und die Kunstauffassung der frühen Romantik* (Darmstadt, 1983). Berglinger is a composer who is gradually destroyed by his increasingly brilliant music. Finally, his Easter music is so intense that it kills him. This Icharus-like notion of art is typical of early German romanticism.

41. See, too, Otto Rank, *Art and Artist: Creative Urge and Personality Development* (New York, 1932).

spiders produce their web, as a purely individual production from within. The anxiety about having an original idea stolen hides the larger fear that there is no such thing as originality—but merely the appearance of it. In Descartes's fear of a genius tempting him from the outside, and in Freud's protoromantic notion of genius as something coming from within, the assumptions concerning creativity and its connection to identity are the same.[42]

The problem of gender lurks here also. The plagiarized text itself is a feminized object, that which is kidnapped and, Helen-like, forced into another's camp. The feminine and its connection to knowledge are already deeply implicated in both of the philosophies considered here: Descartes likens science to a woman, just as Freud endows the unconscious with feminine attributes. Both science and a woman are "mysterious" and need to be "conquered" (Descartes); both woman and the unconscious are enigmas which must be "solved" and, like the dark continent to which they are compared, charted (Freud). Moreover, there is something about feminizing an idea that seems to be contagious. Either the author actively (= masculine) determines where the "womanly" is in his work (as with Descartes and Freud, who openly declare where they see the feminine); or, as we shall see later in this study, the author himself is considered to be afflicted with the feminine ailment, especially when he is identified with his text.[43] In the second instance, femininity is no longer something the (male) author will name and conquer, but rather that element about his work which is passive and unproductive. But we will return to this problem.

There is, of course, the other side of plagiarism: the one who does the thieving is just as entangled in the originality and iden-

42. G. W. Pigman III notes a curious phenomenon in Renaissance texts on imitation: citing Macrobius's excuse for copying others, Pigman points out that "borrowing and its unscrupulous cousin, theft, like culling flowers, are frequent images of nontransformative imitation or following." "Versions of Imitation in the Renaissance," *Renaissance Quarterly* 33, no. 1 (1980): 5. Thus, ironically, the organicist symbol of original genius, the plant, is also a frequent presence in metaphors about theft. This perhaps adds yet another facet to the "Botanical monograph dream."

43. A notion akin to Lacan's idea that the signifier determines the subject under its influence. In "The Seminar on the Purloined Letter," that signifier is feminine, and so feminizes everybody in its path. For the English version of that seminar, translated by Jeffrey Mehlman, see *Yale French Studies*, no. 48 (1972).

tity game as is the one who is robbed. Indeed, to be accused of plagiarizing is in some cases to be even more personally violated than to be plagiarized—and this is true, significantly, whether one has in fact committed the robbery or not. Whether the accused is innocent or guilty, his or her identity (as an original mind, as an author, as a possible "genius") is dramatically at stake. The idea of "originality" makes either end of plagiarism a dangerous one; for the fiction of, and insistence on, "originality" are simultaneously and insolubly at endless play.

Originality puts identity at stake; but in an age (by which I mean the second half of the twentieth century) when the subject itself is constantly in question as an autonomous notion, the idea of originality seems to take on an even greater urgency. These are the issues to be discussed in relation to Paul Celan, the Holocaust poet who is accused one day of plagiarism.

APPENDIX:
DESCARTES'S THREE DREAMS

First Dream

Several phantoms presented themselves and frightened Descartes. Walking through the streets, he had to turn to the left side to move toward the place he wanted to go to, because he felt a great feebleness on the right side, on which he couldn't support himself. Ashamed of walking this way, he tried to straighten himself, but an impetuous wind carried him in a sort of whirlwind and whirled him about three or four times on his left foot. At each step he thought he would fall, until, having seen an open college on the road, he entered, in search of a retreat and remedy for his sickness. He wanted to go in, thinking primarily of prayer; however, having passed a man he knew without greeting him, he tried to retrace his steps to do so but was pushed violently by the wind against the Church. In the middle of the college court he saw another person, who called him courteously by name and told him that if he was looking for Monsieur N., he had something to give him. Descartes imagined it was a melon that had been brought from a foreign country. What surprised him more was to see that those who were gathered around this person stood firm on their feet, while he always remained bent and unsteady. Meanwhile, the wind subsided. He then awoke, and felt a real pain, which made him fear that some evil genius had tried to seduce him. He had been sleeping on his left side, and turned to the right, praying God to save him from misfortune and punishment of his sins.

Second Dream

He had fallen asleep after meditating for two hours on the good and evil of this world. Then he dreamed that he heard a sharp, piercing noise, which he took for a peal of thunder. The fright awoke him, and he perceived sparks of fire all over the room. This had often happened to him before. He would wake up in the middle of the night, quite dazzled. But this time he desired philosophical reasons, and he drew conclusions favorable to his mind.

Third Dream

This dream was not accompanied by feelings of anxiety. In the dream, Descartes found a book on the table, opened it, discovered it was a dictionary, and was delighted with it. Then, that very instant, he found his hand on another book, and did not know where it came from. He ascertained it was an anthology of poems of various authors entitled CORPUS POETARUM. He was curious to read something, and, at the beginning of the book, happened upon the verse, *Quod vitae sectabor iter?* At the same time he saw a man he didn't know but who presented him with a verse beginning *Est et Non,* which he praised. Descartes told him he knew what it was, and that it was one of the Idylls of Ausonius found in the large collection of poets on the table. He wished to show it himself to this man, and began to leaf through the book whose order and arrangement he had boasted he knew perfectly. While he was looking for the place, the man asked him where he had obtained the book, and Descartes answered that he was unable to tell him, but that a moment before he had been holding another one, which had disappeared without his knowing who had brought it or taken it back from him. He hadn't finished when he saw the book appear once more at the other end of the table. But he discovered that this dictionary was not complete as it had been when he saw it the first time. However, in perusing the anthology of poets, he came upon the poems of Ausonius; but not finding the piece which began with *Est et Non,* he told the man he knew another one by the same poet, which was still more beautiful than the former and began *Quod vitae sectabor iter?* The person asked him to show it to him, and Descartes set about looking for it, whereupon he found several small portraits engraved in copperplate; this made him say that the book was very beautiful, but that it was not of the same printing as the one he had known. There he was when the books and the man disappeared and faded from his imagination, without reawakening him.

What was singular in the circumstances of the dream, continues the account, was that "Descartes, wondering whether what he had just seen was a dream or vision, not only decided that it was a dream but rendered its interpretation even before he awoke. He judged that the dictionary represented all the sciences gathered together; and that the anthology of poems, entitled CORPUS POETARUM, indicated particularly, and in a distinct fashion, Philosophy and Wisdom joined together. For he believed one shouldn't be much surprised to see that the poets, even those who fool their time away, have many maxims that are deeper, more sensible, and better expressed than those found in the writings of philosophers. He attributed this wonder to the divinity of Enthusiasm and the force of Imagination, which emitted the seeds of wisdom (found in the minds of all men, like the sparks of fire in flintstones) with much more ease and brilliance than even Reason can do among the philosophers. Descartes, continuing to interpret the dream in his sleep, thought the verse on the uncertainty of the way of life one must choose, which begins with *Quod vitae sectabor iter,* marked the sound advice of a wise person, or even of Moral Theology.

"Thereupon, uncertain whether he was seeing or imagining, he awoke without emotion and, his eyes open, continued to interpret his dream along the same line. By the poets gathered in the anthology he understood Revelation and Enthusiasm, which he hoped would still favor him. By the piece of verse *Est et Non,* which is the Yes and No of Pythagoras, he understood Truth and Falsehood in human knowledge and the secular sciences. Seeing that his work in all these fields was succeeding so well, he was bold enough to persuade himself that it was the Spirit of Truth which had wished to open for him (by this dream) the treasures of all the sciences. There was left for him only to explain the little portraits in copperplate, which he had found in the second book. He didn't try to explain this any more after an Italian painter visited him the next day.

"This last dream, which was altogether very pleasant and agreeable, indicated to him the future and what must happen to him for the rest of his life. But he took the two preceding ones as threatening warnings concerning his past life, which may not have been as innocent before God as before men. And he believed that it was the reason for the terror and fright with which these two dreams had been accompanied. The melon, which was offered him in the first dream, signified, he said, the charms of solitude, but available through purely human attractions. The wind which pushed him towards the Church of the college, when he felt bad on the right side, was nothing but the evil Genius which tried to throw him by force into a place he had voluntarily planned to go."

2

Paul Celan and
the Death of the Book

When we are praising Plato, it seems we are praising quotations from Solon, and Sophron, and Philolaus. Be it so. Every book is a quotation; and every house is a quotation out of all forests, and mines, and stone quarries; and every man is a quotation from all his ancestors.

—EMERSON, "Plato or the Philosopher"

Il est certain que la nation juive est la plus singulière qui jamais ait été dans le monde. Quoiqu'elle soit la plus méprisable aux yeux de la politique, elle est, à bien des égards, considérable aux yeux de la philosophie.

—VOLTAIRE, *Dictionnaire philosophique,* s.v. "Juifs"

A S IF IN RESPONSE to Heidegger, Paul Celan writes that with the German lyric it is never language itself that is operative "but always an 'I' who speaks from the particular angle of reflection which is his existence."[1] This orientation differentiated the German lyric in Celan's eyes from the French, more precisely from the lyric of Mallarmé, which attempts the elocutionary disappearance of the speaking "I." For Celan, poetry is finally the place of the "I," but above all it is, precisely, a *place*. This notion of poetry as a place, and as the last place of the "I," is specifically related to the issues of creativity and identity which we have been considering. Place itself should be understood here as a specific concept.

1. Response to a questionnaire sent by the Librairie Flinker in 1961. In *Paul Celan's Collected Prose,* trans. Rosemary Waldrop (Manchester, 1986), p. 16. Hereafter abbreviated as *CP.*

Michel de Certeau has contributed brilliantly to the place of *place* in history, arguing that any social analysis is impossible without it. Denial of place, he argues, is the principle of ideology, and excludes theory: "Even more, by moving discourse into a non-place, ideology forbids history from speaking of society and of death—in other words, from being history."[2] The way I am using the notion of place here should be seen in Certeau's terms, but modified: the Holocaust destroys historical place for Celan. The text itself will serve as place, and as the place as well for the rehistoricization and the fragile rehypostatization of a notion of the subject. Just as social analysis is impossible without place, so too is any speaking subject at all—including the subject that argues against its own autonomy or perpetrates its own critique.

Lyric poetry is commonly seen as the site of a poetic self, of the first person pronoun, and so on; but when Celan says that poetry is the place of the "I," his statement is to be understood literally. There is no other place for him, and no other "I." Indeed, it may be that a project such as Mallarmé's—the attempt to erase the speaking subject from lyric poetry—is possible only in a historical situation which so privileges the individual that the subject can afford the luxury of risking itself, as it were, textually. For Celan, however, the problem is quite the reverse: how to reimagine the speaking "I" when it has been eradicated by history, and when it has only the text left where it is perhaps not entirely erased.

I am not disagreeing here with Foucault's argument that the self is a historical construct; quite the contrary. We can agree with Foucault that disciplinary power creates the emergence of the modern individual, working to make that individual both an object of scrutiny and in instrument of its exercise. As Foucault notes, power does not mean strength but, rather, the specific relation that power has to knowledge in a given society.[3] But the survivor of the Holocaust has witnessed the eradication not only of the individual but of the history of society as it had been un-

2. Michel de Certeau, *The Writing of History,* trans. Tom Conley (New York, 1988), p. 69.
3. See, for example, Foucault's "The Subject and Power," in *Michel Foucault: Beyond Structuralism and Hermeneutics,* ed. Hubert L. Dreyfus and Paul Rabinow (Chicago, 1982).

derstood. That is, the survivor must face the objectification of the individual by an ideology which does more than demonstrate the relation between knowledge and power. If we combine the thinking of Certeau and Foucault for our present purposes, we may say, on the one hand, that the ideology of the Third Reich returns to pre-eighteenth-century Europe, when, as Foucault says, power was manifest and those who did not have it lurked in its shadows, unsure of their existence as individuals, not to mention as "selves."[4] On the other hand, the Holocaust promoted an ideology which moved discourse to what Certeau calls a non-place. The consequences of manifest power were hidden even from its victims; millions of deaths remained unspoken, forbidden topics. History could not be history; natural law was pushed aside to remove a basis for condemnation. It is my contention here that the reinscription of the subject which Celan attempts in his texts can only be understood in the context of the obscenity the Holocaust visits upon the individual's idea of the value of human life, and of him- or herself as a part of that life. The Holocaust functions as a new kind of upheaval for the notion of the individual: the individual is left searching for a self and a voice by which to describe its own obliteration.

Thus the question of the status of the subject is essential to any approach to Celan's verse. More particularly, Celan's poetry forces the issue of a textually constructed "I." The problem of the textual "I" has been much discussed, of course, in critical theory and philosophy. Let us consider, somewhat at random, a few contrasting notions of the subject's place in the text. In his study of the problem in three poets, including Celan, John Jackson unsurprisingly notes that there is more to the first person singular than just its articulation: "If the subject needs a grammatical form," he says, "he will need, for the form to become act, the extralinguistic possibility of its affirmation."[5] Or, as Paul Ricoeur puts it, to say "this" (*ceci*) is meaningless unless it points to something outside

---

4. See Foucault's *Madness and Civilization: A History of Insanity in the Age of Reason* (New York, 1965). See also Foucault's work on the birth of clinics, prisons, and insane asylums.

5. John Jackson, *La question du moi: un aspect de la modernité poétique européenne: T. S. Eliot, Paul Celan, Yves Bonnefoy* (Neuchâtel, 1978), p. 13; my translation.

of itself.[6] For both Jackson and Ricoeur, the textual subject must exist in relation to the world, to a place outside the text, in order to *be*.

For Hans Georg Gadamer, the lyrical "I" is a fisherman who throws out a net to catch a poem. His book on Celan begins with that metaphor. To the difficult questions he chooses to ask of Celan's verse, "Who is speaking? About whom are we speaking?" he answers with an optimistic "That is what we are here to learn" (*Wir haben es zu lernen*).[7] His approach, in other words, will answer the questions it poses. It will situate Celan's "I" in a hermeneutical, classical tradition even as Gadamer himself will claim to have no time for those who say they "understand" Celan. For Gadamer, the dialogue itself has a "thou" whose identification precedes discourse. But such an assumption—of an a priori thou and "I"—largely disqualifies Gadamer from any reading of Celan's speaking subject. For Celan's subject does not, precisely, precede its textual presence; it is born into it—or, more precisely, its obliteration can be articulated only in the text.

The question of Celan's textual "I" has, predictably, been frequently linked to Buber's I and Thou; partly because the Thou (Du) is everywhere, partly because Celan favors the dialogue, and partly because Buber shares Celan's conviction that all art is encounter. But for Buber, dialogue is a way to God; for Celan, poetic speech is the only basis for existence. It is the only *place* left for existence.

For Celan, poetry is place and world, and none of the critical works mentioned will help us in approaching his speaking subject. There are no mixed horizons or a priori "Thous" (Gadamer), no available outside world (Ricoeur, Jackson), no project of pure

6. See, e.g., Paul Ricoeur, "The Question of the Subject," in *The Conflict of Interpretations* (Evanston, 1974), pp. 236–66. Here, too, Ricoeur reminds us that for psychoanalysis such notions as conscious, preconscious, and unconscious are *places*. See also Ricoeur, *Oneself as Another*, trans. Kathleen Blamey (Chicago, 1992), especially pp. 56ff.

7. Hans Georg Gadamer, *Wer bin ich und wer bist du? Ein Kommentar zu Paul Celans Gedichtfolge "Atemkristall"* (Frankfurt a.M., 1973), p. 13. For a recent analysis of conversation, see David Tracy's wonderful *Plurality and Ambiguity: Hermeneutics, Religion, Hope* (San Francisco, 1987), especially the first chapter. For an examination of Gadamer on conversation, see Joel C. Weisheimer, *Gadamer's Hermeneutics: A Reading of Truth and Method* (New Haven, 1985), pp. 325–45.

poetry (Mallarmé). Celan's subject is lost, not a given to be questioned or upheld. Thus agency is lost, for it can only be present where, as in Descartes, there is an a priori existence of the subject as a reflexive mediation.

It is in these terms that I believe we must understand what poetry is for Celan. This poetry does not seek to be "transcendent"; rather, it strains to be concrete, like a handshake, like a message in a bottle (the analogies are Celan's). It does not stand in for the world; it is neither metaphor, nor a form of agency, nor an attempt to retrieve what has been lost. It is simply the only place upon which to stand and speak. But this does not imply that when Celan writes "I," he means himself. Hegel, in the *Phenomenology of the Spirit,* argues that to understand man by understanding his origin is the same as understanding the origin of the "I" revealed by speech. For Celan, the text is origin's diaspora; it affords him a minimal ground on which he can speak for a dispossessed subject, and at times *as if* (*als ob*) a subject. And this aspect of Celan manifests itself literally, concretely. As his belief in the word lessened, so the actual length of his lines of verse shortened and splintered. His terrain, which was his verse, was shrinking and becoming increasingly unstable. "Language belongs to the closest neighborhood of man's being," notes Heidegger, the philosopher with whom Celan had felt a kinship. Heidegger adds, "Language is the precinct (*templum*), that is, the house of Being."[8] The philosopher's metaphors are, not insignificantly, the poet's reality.

It is the Holocaust which destroys place for Celan, as we have already said. Place, however, obviously engages notions not only of history and society but also of property, of possession. Lewis Hyde notes that an old definition of property calls it a "right of action." He explains: "To possess, to enjoy, to use, to destroy, to sell, to rent, to give or bequeath, to improve, to pollute—all of these are actions, and a thing (or a person) becomes a 'property' whenever someone has 'in it' the right of any such action. There is no property without an actor, then, and in this sense property

8. From Martin Heidegger, *Poetry, Language, Thought,* trans. Albert Hofstadter (New York, 1975), pp. 189, 132.

is an expression of the human will in things (and in other people)."[9] I am provisionally using this definition, among the many (and far more technical) available, because it both clarifies and inadvertently demonstrates the problem. In the first place, it makes clear that property entails someone who is able to act upon something. Such an action therefore assumes an autonomous subject, who has (again, literally) ground from which or on which to act. But it is clear that Hyde is having problems with the notion "person" in relation to such action. "There is no property without an actor" also means that there is no person without property. The word "things," moreover, keeps getting qualified by "or people"—a crucial ambiguity. Here we have the material, legal ramifications of the more metaphysical concerns we have been considering. For in society a human being does not, in fact, seem to be a person at all unless he or she *owns* rather than *is* property. We are already encountering the cliché of the active/masculine equation versus the passive/feminine referred to in the previous chapter, an issue to which we shall return later in this study. What matters at this point is that property engenders personhood and identity; that to have rights of action, one needs to own. It goes without saying that in this sense, among countless others, the Holocaust destroys personhood for its survivors.

Edmond Jabès has remarked that territory and property (and therefore, by implication, personhood) has long been a problematic issue for "the Jew," the term he and other postmodern Jewish writers use.[10] I take their use of this term to be more than a

---

9. Lewis Hyde, *The Gift: Imagination and the Erotic Life of Property* (New York, 1979), p. 94.

10. In *Heidegger and 'the jews'*, trans. Andreas Michel and Mark Roberts (Minneapolis, 1990), Jean-François Lyotard argues for the use of the term "the jews": "I make it plural to signify that it is neither a figure nor a political (Zionism), religious (Judaism) or philosophical (Jewish philosophy) subject. I put quotation marks to avoid confusing these 'jews' with real Jews. What is most real about the real Jews is that Europe, in any case, does not know what to do with them . . . 'the jews' are the object of a dismissal with which Jews, in particular, are afflicted in reality" (p. 3). Lyotard insists that "the jews" are not to be confused with "real Jews." Nevertheless, as David Carroll notes in his introduction to the English translation of this work, it is impossible to dissociate the two. The tradition and ethics of the Jews with which "the jews" are linked here are largely the influence of Levinas on Lyotard, through whom he reads them. Thus the term "the jews," is in Kantian terms not a representation, but a *factum;* something to be remembered as that which never ceases to be forgotten. By "the jews," Lyotard wants to

reference to a historical reality, more than a trope. The term also functions at another level: the idea of "the Jew" as someone by definition without personhood or property is born of the Diaspora, and is a minority discourse in a particular manner that I hope to make clear. That is not to say that such a discourse is not a reality for those, like Celan, who espouse it. Quite the contrary: it is in the nature of minority discourse to assume the language and stance of the oppressor, such that the view of "the Jew" as marginalized, for example, becomes a viable given.[11] Thus the "majority" notion that "the Jew" is not a person and has no rights (including

mean Jews and non-Jews jointly responsible for articulating the place of radical alterity in critical discourse. In spite of Lyotard's debt to Levinas, I read *Heidegger and 'the jews'* as an attempt to understand alterity itself (as that which is never comprehended, or as the limits of the subject's ability to understand its own notion of what is marginalized in Western thought). The book is more metaphysically oriented (deconstruction, the place of Heidegger in Western philosophy) than political, although I agree with Carroll that it is more political than it acknowledges. Given that, Lyotard is not using the term "the jews" in quite the same way as is Celan and the writers mentioned here.

I purposely use "the Jews" with an uppercase *J* in order to emphasize the politically specific sense in which I understand it to be used by Levinas, Steiner, and other postmodern Jewish writers, many of whom I mention here. There are moments, moreover, when even Lyotard approaches the minority discourse (in my sense), which he generally succeeds in undermining. For example: "Every Jew is a bad 'jew,' a bad witness to what cannot be represented, just like all texts fail to reinscribe what has not been inscribed" (p. 81). This is clearly meant to be *erlebte Rede;* but its oracular tone, coupled with its scriberly metaphors, derive as much from the assumptions inherent in the discourse of a Celan, as from a debt to Levinas. Thus the ambiguity which Lyotard chooses in his notion of "the jews" allows for placing him in two frequently opposing positions, each with its own discourse: the consciously minor, criticizing, marginalized position (one which seeks to include the excluders as well as the excluded in the margin, with the term "the jews," and successfully undertakes a critique of radical alterity as seen by the hegemonic culture); but also the position of a minority discourse, which (unconsciously) sees itself in terms chosen by the dominant culture. Thus the *erlebte Rede,* normally a tool of irony demonstrating the author's control over his subject, here becomes a dangerous moment where the text risks a fissure. Who is it who feels that "every Jew is a bad 'jew'," when the term "jew" is already given to us by Lyotard himself? What is the irony? And on whose ground is Lyotard standing? These are the dangers inherent in the willed ambiguity with which Lyotard aligns himself in his book.

11. I am generally using "minority discourse" in a way similar to what is called "minor literature" by G. Deleuze and Guattari in *Kafka: Toward a Minor Literature,* trans. Dana Polan (Minneapolis, 1986). That book argues that a natural territory gives a natural frame to literature; that minority literature must establish a place for itself, given that such a literature is what they call "deterritorialized." Most of the traits which, according to the authors, characterize minor literature are applicable to Celan: writing in a language not your own, for example; being in exile; belonging to a marginalized group; and so on. But whereas Deleuze and Guattari

property rights) is integrated into the very discourse which seeks to rectify the anti-Semitism from which such views originate. This is the case even in the rich and complex texts of those twentieth-century Jewish writers whom Celan admired, some of whom will be cited here alongside others with whom he was not familiar.

Such an identification with the oppressor's view of "the Jew," I believe, largely creates the tragedy to be discussed here. It is in the nature of minor literature, as David Lloyd notes, to refuse to reterritorialize identity.[12] And yet, in a sense, this is precisely what Celan was attempting to do. We might term his minority discourse one which seeks reterritorialization with a lucid conviction that it is unattainable. It is a discourse telling of the failure, not the refusal, to reterritorialize, which distinguishes it from consciously minor literature in Guattari and Deleuze's sense. Far from being refused, reterritorialization is endlessly mourned.

---

see in "minor literature" a consciously disruptive element within the fabric of the dominant culture, "minority discourse," as I use it, is as marginalized as minor literature but (unconsciously) sees itself in the dominant culture's terms. In this sense, George Steiner's view that "the Jew" should always wander serves as an example of "minority discourse." Celan speaks from within a minority discourse which, while it does not try to homogenize itself into the dominant culture (in his case, French, Catholic, European, bourgeois, and so on), is conscious neither of its view of itself nor of the extent of the dominant culture's legacy in that view. Yet the minority discourse, though frequently grounded on many of the assumptions of the oppressor or of the hegemony, is also capable—perhaps in spite of itself—of being as disruptive, as scandalous, and as inapplicable to pre-existing models as is minor literature itself. As with minor literature, everything about minority discourse is ultimately political, whether openly so or not. For a historical overview of the role of language, reading, and text in the Diaspora, see Benjamin Harshav's *The Meaning of Yiddish* (Berkeley and Los Angeles, 1990), pp. 15ff. Harshav emphasizes several "traits" of Jewish society in the Diaspora, based on its (masculinist) culture of studying holy text: that it was "book oriented," given to questioning, and emphasized dialogue (which will eventually be "canonized as text" in the form of the Talmud). "What was canonized in Judaism," writes Harshav, "was the biblical *text*, not necessarily its specific *meanings*" (p. 16; emphasis his). Thus these tendencies, as Harshav convincingly traces them, share some common thread with what I am calling the minority discourse on "the Jew": the importance of the book *as* book, the sacredness of language (Yiddish the mother tongue, Hebrew the Holy Tongue—terms that Celan himself uses), the great extent to which text and everyday life were interwoven in many contexts of the Diaspora. The minority discourse does not spring ex nihilo; but its consequences for the post-Holocaust are what I am trying to get at here.

12. David Lloyd, "Genet's Genealogy: European Minorities and the End of the Canon," the first of two special issues of *Cultural Critique*, nos. 6 and 7 (Spring and Fall 1987), on "The Nature and Context of Minority Discourse," ed. Abdul R. JanMohamed and David Lloyd.

Thus Celan's discourse both insists upon its status as minor (suspicious of narrative, of representations of identity, of unification and reconciliation) and simultaneously sees itself as a minority in the given terms of the hegemonic culture. Hence both the power and the tragedy of such a discourse.

The Jew makes the book into his territory, says Jabès, since he has none otherwise in the Diaspora. The book is his homeland in exile. Therefore, he says, being Jewish necessarily means being a writer; the Jew reads rather than lives his life: "Deprived of freedom, deprived of a territory, it was natural that the Jew should take refuge in the book which immediately became the lasting place his freedom could resort to." (Here too, the word "place" is significant.)[13] Judaism is the act of writing, adds Derrida, who cites Levinas. There is no Jewish property: "the Jew is the other who has no essence . . . ; the Jew, the name Jew, is a *Shibboleth*."[14] George Steiner, in an article significantly entitled "Our Homeland, the Text," claims that "the text is home; each commentary a return."[15] The poet is the subject of the book, in both senses. And thus all poets are Jews, says Marina Tsvetayeva, in her epigram for Celan's poem "And with the Book from Tarussa." The post-Holocaust Jewish writer, especially one who remains in the Diaspora, returns to the text twice dispossessed of property: first by virtue of frequently seeing him- or herself from within the bounds of a discourse which necessarily binds "the Jew" to the status of otherness and to a place described as exile, never home; second by having had the land acquired in the adopted country taken away. By contrast, the book, at least on the surface, seems a safe haven.

Yet the book itself is neither safe nor the Jew's property: "What does [the Jew] have," Celan asks, "that is really his own, that is not borrowed, taken and not returned?" For the book is communal—it does not belong to a single individual; it is not, in this sense, private property. It belongs to "the Jew," not to a particular Jew. We are back at the problem of property and identity, a com-

---

13. *Midrash and Literature,* ed. Geoffrey H. Hartman and Sanford Budick (New Haven, 1986), p. 358.

14. Jacques Derrida, "Shibboleth," in ibid., p. 338.

15. *Salmagundi,* no. 66 (Winter–Spring 1985), p. 7.

bination peculiarly European—not, in other words, specifically "the Jew's" problem.

John Locke's *Two Treatises on Government* (1690) are the paradigm of the European notion that an individual's work and the fruit of his labor are his own property (I use the masculine pronoun here purposefully, for obvious historical reasons). This assertion was based on the then-surprising declaration that every man owns his body and is therefore his own person: "Though the Earth, and all inferior Creatures be common to all Men, yet every Man has a *Property* in his own *Person*. This no Body has any Right to but himself. The *Labour* of his Body, and the *Work* of his hands, we may say, are properly his. Whatsoever then he removes out of the State that Nature hath provided, and left it in, he hath mixed his *Labour* with, and joyned to it something that is his own, and thereby makes it his property."[16] This remarkable statement not only delineates a tenet central to modern European thought, but also prepares the way for any charge of plagiarism. Literature is a form of labor and, as such, becomes personal property much as the product of any field or territory. It is such think-

16. John Locke, *Two Treatises on Government*, ed. Peter Laslett (Cambridge, 1963), pp. 305–6. Lewis Hyde, in *The Gift*, points out that a body ceased being property by law at death: "The law recognized no property rights in the body. Growing out of a religious sense of the sacredness of the body, this legal formula was intended to make it clear that executors of an estate could not make the body of the deceased into an item of commerce to be bought, sold, or used to pay debts." This situation has changed entirely, however, with the advent of organ transplants: "As soon as it became possible to transplant an organ from the dead to the living, however, it became clear that the sense of 'property rights' being used here was too vague. The law justly restrained the right to sell, but what of the right to bestow?" (pp. 94–95). This state of affairs is further complicated by high-tech science's recent ability to "clone" human tissue. For example, in 1988 John Moore sued for profits (evidently in the form of royalties) from the use of what seemed a valuable cell line derived from his spleen. As *Bio/Technology* (October 1988) puts it, doctors are now saddled with the burden of obtaining informed consent in these matters "before a court has even established whether a patient *has* a property right to removed tissues." Companies that want to use such cell lines developed by third parties for their new products must now also worry about "warranties and good titles." So much for the sacredness of the body and the legal attempts to prevent executors of estates from turning the body into an item of commerce. The body has become the person in such commodification (or vice versa). In the case of Moore, the cell line was called "Mo." The article in *Bio/Technology* notes that Moore's doctor met his patient socially enough times to begin calling him "Mo," "as if the cell line and the patient were one and the same." To such science fictions are added things like a patented mouse (Harvard's) and, for example, a patented algorithm.

ing which allows for the notion of author: the word "author" derives from the Latin *augere,* meaning to increase, augment, grow (terms of cultivation, work, and so on). There is no author without first a concept of personal property and hence of person.[17] An author's text is *like* a piece of land, and he has first rights to its harvest.

But although the author owns his text, he cannot own the words, since they belong to everybody. And how can an idea be property, since it is intangible? So, as we have noted, the territory of the book, that homeland in exile which the Jew has sought for himself, is already a tenuous holding in this European exile.

In his speech accepting the Büchner prize, Celan says he is searching for his "place of origin" but cannot find it on any map. "None of these places can be found," he says; "They do not exist." In the same speech, he calls an estrangement from the "I" a freedom, one he wants to have located as *place:* "Can we perhaps now locate the strangeness, the place where the person was able to set himself free as an estranged—I? Can we locate this place, this step?" (*CP,* p. 46).[18] Indeed, Celan had said, the Jew seems to have nothing that is not borrowed. Further, the Jew and nature are strangers to each other, Celan continues. What is earthy and material is language, not ground; what is cultivated is text, not crops. The text is the ground upon which the Jew stands to say "I" and from which to say "Thou." But even this ground is borrowed. Within this discourse, the situation of the European Jew, with respect to the text, to private property, and to the European notion of "person," is already extremely difficult, and self-consciously so. From this perspective, even "the Jew's" personhood is borrowed.

Tenuous as the ground of the text may be, there can be no real exile from the book or from writing. The body itself is written—

17. Michel de Certeau has pointed out, however, that the present notion of *auctoritas* has shifted from author to expert (e.g., the Rembrandt Commission, which decides what "is" and "is not" an original, bonafide, acknowledged Rembrandt). *Heterologies: Discourse on the Other,* trans. Brian Massumi, Theory and History of Literature, 17 (Minneapolis and Oxford, 1986).

18. For James Clifford, the problem articulated here by Celan belongs to modernity, which Clifford sees as synonymous with rootlessness (or "poetics of displacement," as he also calls it). See Clifford, *The Predicament of Culture: Twentieth-century Ethnography, Literature, and Art* (Cambridge, MA, 1988).

as in Psalm 139, "In thy book, all my members were written."
Only the poem, Celan says, can create a topography, or a geography, a "space of conversation" which can establish "the naming
and speaking I." The origin of any notion of the subject is always
the text. Further, the I always brings "its otherness into the
poem." The poem itself searches for "open, empty free space."
Celan's poetic "I" moves toward being a poem, just as his poem
moves toward having a space, a territory at least provisionally its
own. What Celan writes of the poet Osip Mandelstam describes
his own project as well: "[He] made the poem into a place where
all we can perceive and attain through language is gathered
around a centre which provides form and truth, around the existence of an individual who challenges the hour . . . ; this is to
show how much Mandelstam's poems, risen out of the ruin of a
ruined man, are relevant to us today" (*CP*, 17). Celan, too, makes
the poem into a place; but, for many of the Jewish writers whom
Celan read, language and poetry were already the homeland. As
we shall see, the tropes and notions of poetry that Celan uses not
only echo many of the Jewish writers writing just before and
after the Holocaust—those who write in what we have referred
to as a minority discourse; more cruelly, but not coincidentally,
they also are in unison with some of Heidegger's ideas on the role
of poetry in the world.[19] Heidegger's is, of course, the discourse
of the oppressor. Celan's identification with the philosopher's
views on poetry could be said to be the logical, intellectual (almost hermeneutical) extension of the politics of any minority discourse, which always (unconsciously) strains to adopt the language and perspective of the oppressor.

The Holocaust destroys the Diaspora homeland and destroys,
quite literally, the book as well. (In an ironic twist, right after the
war Celan got a job burning Russian books.) But it also destroys
the place from which the speaking subject can begin its discourse,
its own critique. "Disaster [*le désastre*]," Maurice Blanchot writes,
"does not put me into question, but lifts the question, makes it
disappear. It is as if the 'I' disappeared with it into the disaster

19. For example, in "What are Poets For?" in Heidegger, *Poetry, Language,
Thought*. Heidegger reads Rilke in frequently identical terms.

without appearance. The fact of disappearing is precisely not a fact, an event; it does not happen, not only because—and this follows from the supposition itself—there is no 'I' to undergo the experience, but because experience itself is unimaginable."[20] The courage it took for Celan to rewrite himself—or, at least, to rewrite a "speaking, naming I"—into a homeland-text is immeasurable, especially in light of Adorno's pronouncement that after Auschwitz all poetry is barbaric. Adorno later revised this view, at least with respect to Celan (to whom he was not specifically referring, he claimed, in the first place). With Celan, Adorno says in *Aesthetic Theory*, poetry becomes something more than the idea that "the only purpose in life was a beautiful verse of a perfect sentence." In Celan, Adorno sees the completion of Baudelaire's task as Benjamin saw it: to write poetry without an aura.[21]

Peter Szondi seems to me much closer to understanding Celan's project than Adorno, with his rather rigid notions about the poem. In response to Adorno's famous interdiction of poetry, Szondi says that after Auschwitz no poem is possible *except* on the basis of Auschwitz.[22] Just as the poetic "I" for Celan always "brings otherness into the present," so after the Holocaust the text becomes the Diaspora from the Diaspora, the exile from exile. At the same time, in this discourse, for "the Jew" there is never a time when the text is left behind. Suffice it to say that the text is as if in ruins, and so rebuilding becomes the focus.[23] After the war, the text for Celan not only is a territory which affords the Jew ground upon which to stand (Jabès, Levinas, Derrida, Szondi, Steiner); it also marks the site where a speaking "I" is searched for through the text. It is the memory of a notion of a sovereign subject at work—a memory which may itself be false. Thus creation for Celan works on several levels, all of them fragile, all of them vital, all of them already doomed.

20. Maurice Blanchot, *L'Ecriture du désastre*, (Paris, 1980) p. 50. My translation.

21. Theodor Adorno, *Aesthetic Theory*, trans. C. Lenhardt, ed. Gretel Adorno and Rolf Tiedemann (New York, 1984), p. 444.

22. Peter Szondi, "Nach Auschwitz ist kein Gedicht mehr möglich, es sei denn auf Grund von Auschwitz." *Celan Studien* (Frankfurt a.M., 1972), pp. 102–3.

23. For an interpretation of the exile's relationship to the "Vaterland," see Ursula Püschel's "Exilierte und Verlorene," in *Kürbiskern: Literatur, Kritik, Klassenkampf*, ed. Hitzer, Neumann, Schuhler, and Stütz, vol. 4 (Munich, 1977), pp. 104–19.

In the poem "No-one's-rose," we read: *niemand bespricht unsern Staub. / Niemand / Gelobt seist du, Niemand* ("No one speaks of our dust. / No one / blessed be thou, No one"). Or: *Wurzel Abrahams. Wurzel Jesse. Niemandes / Wurzel—o / unser* ("Root of Abraham, root of Jesse. No one's / root—oh / ours"). It is no one who will speak; no one having become the only witness left.

Once again it must be stressed that this creation through a negative (not a negation) emphasizes that it is not the recreation of the subject that is undertaken, but a recreation of the notion of the subject from within a discourse that has already marginalized it; of its possibility within the only realm imaginable: the book. Even if, as Levinas says, paraphrasing Celan, it is now a language far removed from the "I-Thou," having become a language of "it and him" which moves endlessly toward the other. "It is a language older than the truth of being," says Levinas [*un langage plus ancien que la vérité de l'être*].[24] The stakes could not be higher.

Celan claimed that all poetry springs from a wound and leads to the rupture of the self within the self, to a splitting, to the summoning (*rufen*) of the Other from within. In this sense too we can understand that he felt close to the writings of Heidegger, for whom pain itself is "dif-ference," tearing, the famous *Riss*.[25] Heidegger's notion that thought is primordially dialogical, that it must return to a dialogue with poetry for thinking to occur, and his endorsement of Hölderlin's remark that all language is a conversation are statements which could, on the surface at least, be attributed to Celan as much as to Heidegger.[26]

For Heidegger, poets name and bring into being; they "capture the world thus opened up." And Heidegger is also, of course, the philosopher who puts the privileging of the subject, which he sees as one of the major tenets of Western metaphysics, into serious question. His famous "Letter on Humanism," refuting Sartre's emphasis on human subjectivity, critiques Cartesian subjectivism as well.[27] I do not wish to argue that Celan was a Heideggerian

24. Emmanuel Levinas, *Noms propres* (Paris, 1976), p. 50.
25. See, e.g., "Language," in Heidegger, *Poetry, Language, Thought.*
26. See Heidegger's "Hölderlin and the Essence of Poetry," in *Existence and Being*, ed. and trans. Werner Brock (Chicago, 1949), pp. 270–91.
27. The "Letter on Humanism" is a response to Sartre's *L'Existentialisme est un humanisme.* Heidegger proposes privileging being rather than subjectivity. Any

or even well versed in the philosopher's ideas. But Celan had read some of the German philosopher's work and knew enough to believe (as did many) that here was a kindred spirit, a philosopher who held that poetry could redeem thought; that subjectivity was at best tenuous; and that Hölderlin (whom Celan admired enormously) was the great poet who, understanding all of this, tried to capture the world and reveal it in its unconcealedness.[28] Indeed, Levinas makes explicit the Heideggerian echoes in Celan's statements about poetry: "[Celan] tells us how little understanding he has for a certain language that posits the world in being, as significant as the burst of the *physis* for the pre-Socratics."[29]

How then could a philosopher such as Heidegger have been connected with the Nazis? In 1967 Celan went to Heidegger's home at Todtnauberg, in the Black Forest, to ask him, essentially, why he kept silent about the extent of his connection to the Nazis. That meeting has prompted a number of essays by critics, especially in the 1980s when Heidegger's Nazi sympathies received much scrutiny.[30] In all of these essays, one senses the at-

---

privileging of the subject splits *physis* from *logos* which then becomes the *ratio* of Descartes.

28. Kathleen Mullaney has shown that this "conversation" between poetry and thought is an illusory dialectic, or dialogue, since Heidegger makes clear that it is philosophy that decides which poetry is "great" and is therefore admissible into such an encounter in the first place. See Mullaney's Ph.D. dissertation, "René Char and Heidegger: The Encounter of Poetry and Thought" (University of Chicago, 1992).

29. Levinas, *Noms propres,* p. 50. "[Celan] nous dit le peu de compréhension qu'il a pour une certaine langue qui instaure le monde dans l'être, signifiante comme l'éclat de la *physis* des présocratiques."

30. E.g., Philippe Lacoue-Labarthe, *La poésie comme expérience* (Paris, 1986), who argues that Celan's poetry is "toute entière un dialogue avec la *pensée* de Heidegger" (p. 50) and who compares him to a wandering Oedipus. Mark Anderson, "Paul Celan and the Impossibility of Poetry" (unpublished) gives a critical reading of Lacoue-Labarthe's own reading of the meeting with Heidegger. Anderson quite properly reminds us that Celan, unlike Heidegger, does not see the poem as standing outside of time; it stands "across time, not above it" (p. 15). For an overview (albeit a biased one, which makes it all the more interesting) on the place of Heidegger in France, see Jean Beaufret, "Heidegger vu de France," first published in Heidelberg in 1969 and reprinted in Beaufret, *De l'existentialisme à Heidegger* (Paris, 1986). Beaufret, the French apologist of Heidegger, argues that the French "resistance" to Heidegger stems from the fact that, for the French, Husserl must be seen as a modern thinker. They therefore resist Heidegger's notion that phenomenology is rooted in Greek thought.

Heidegger chose silence in general concerning his involvement in Nazi politics.

tempt to come to terms either with Heidegger for his politics or with Celan for his Heideggerian moments. Not surprisingly, the connection and, even more, the meeting between the two men have something disturbing about them. Part of the disturbance may stem from the implications of Celan's initial attraction to Heidegger's views: from within the minority discourse that Celan almost automatically assumes, the German philosopher's views are seductive: they represent, as I have said, a certain language of the dominant, which is seductive on more than the metaphysical or poetic level. The espousal of this dominant discourse has particular importance for a poet who defines himself as "the Jew," a term Heidegger understands as requiring no quotation marks.

In any case, Heidegger kept his silence. Celan might have answered his own question with the piece he had written eight years earlier, "Conversation in the Mountains." Two Jews meet in the mountains, but the text ends with the words "me on the way to myself, up here." Or, as Celan later put it himself, "it was myself I encountered there." Every poem is an encounter, Celan had claimed, and it is part of the tenuousness of the self that it encounters itself as other.[31] The reverse can also occur, however: the encounter with Heidegger produced a poem, "Todtnauberg," about the failure of the "conversation."[32]

"Todtnauberg" also speaks of a book, the Book. The poet goes to "the Hut," the philosopher's home in the mountains, and asks: "the line / —Whose name did the book / register before mine?—/ the line inscribed / in that book about / a hope, today, / of a thinking man's / coming / word / in the heart." But the thinking man never uttered the word of sorrow that Celan

See, e.g., Avital Ronell's *The Telephone Book: Technology—Schizophrenia—Electronic Speech* (Lincoln, NE, 1989), which discusses Heidegger's interview in *Der Spiegel.*

31. It should be added that this encounter was itself a failure: Celan was to have met Adorno in the mountains, a rendezvous that Celan hinted he was not sorry to have missed. See, e.g., Felstiner, "Paul Celan and the Strain of Jewishness," *Commentary,* April 1985, p. 51.

32. See the appendix to this chapter for the text of the poem. See also Joel Golb, "Celan and Heidegger: A Reading of 'Todtnauberg,'" *Seminar, a Journal of German Studies* 24, no. 3 (September 1988): 255–68. Golb concludes that the poem's last section concerns "the entire pattern of intertextuality between Heidegger and Celan" (p. 265).

longed for. Heidegger, it seems, pretended not to understand Celan's question, and so Celan's hope for a coming word ended. Upon leaving, the poet signed the guest book (a well-known ritual for visitors of Todtnauberg). We do not know what he wrote; we may suppose that he reiterated the still unanswered question. Once more, the book gives Celan ground on which to stand, from which to approach the other, though the enounter itself failed.

But the poet worries about who else is in that book. The poem plays against the image of the Book of God. "Whosoever hath sinned against Me," God tells Moses, "him will I blot out of my book" (Exodus 24:7). And by inversion (a familiar rhetorical figure for Celan, as Hamacher has noted),[33] the poem alters the traditional meaning. For Celan, the Jews have already been blotted out of the Book of Life, of God. By reinscribing himself in Heidegger's book, Celan reinstates the Jew in the text of German thought and, I think he hopes, in the philosopher's conscience.

The philosopher's book is perhaps a book of evil, since the righteous have been blotted out. Who else, Celan worries, has his name in the same pages. In whose company is his name, are his lines, in the book of the German thinker? "Art requires that we travel a certain space in a certain direction, on a certain road," Celan says in "The Meridian" (again, it is art that creates space). At the end of "Todtnauberg," the road turns muddy and unclear: "The half- / trodden fascine / walks over the high moors, / dampness, / much."[34] The direction, the road, and the space have been uncertain with Heidegger. And the ground afforded him by Heidegger's book is, Celan fears, unclean, its tracks unidentifiable. Thus "Todtnauberg" achieves a double twist: place is turned into text; at the same time, the text itself is brought under further suspicion. With muddiness everywhere, it becomes impossible to tell path from filth, and track from randomness. The encounter itself, which Celan saw as one of the graces of poetry, of the world, is being destabilized as an instrument of hope.

The anecdote of Heidegger and the book points to a central

33. Werner Hamacher, "Die Sekunde der Inversion: Bewegungen einer Figur durch Celans Gedichte," in *Paul Celan,* ed. Hamacher and Winfried Menninghaus (Frankfort, 1988), pp. 81–126.
34. Trans. Michael Hamburger, *Poems of Paul Celan* (New York, 1988), p. 293.

moment of crisis in Celan: on the one hand, as I have been stress-
ing, the need for the book as ground, as place, all the more after
the Holocaust—the need to write poetry in the mother tongue.
But on the other hand, the book has expunged not the sinner but
the innocent; it is no longer the same book. Moral retribution
has been transformed into the censorship of human life. And the
mother tongue is also the language of the murderer. So that just
as the speaking "I" immediately conjures up otherness for Celan,
so the German language is always used as if against itself; as if it
were, in fact, a foreign tongue, the language of the other, of the
enemy. The American poet Jed Rasula has said that with Celan
the German language becomes the means of its own disembodi-
ment.[35] There is no belief in communication; hence, poetry is a
message in a bottle, as if for future readers of a different history,
who might understand.

George Steiner contends that "all of Celan's own poetry is
translated *into* German."[36] As if, in other words, the real, unspoken, native tongue were silently lurking beneath the German.
Indeed, Celan's translations are as strange as his own texts. Discussing Celan's translation of Shakespeare, Szondi points to a
self-destructive coexistence with the German language.[37] Steiner
sees the translator as always *en fausse situation,* remaining part
stranger to the translation and part stranger to the original. Since
that metaphor exactly describes Celan's relationship to his
mother tongue, and his view of himself, it is hardly surprising
that he was such a good translator. Perhaps this is why Celan
critics center on translations of his verse, or his translations of
others. Such a *fausse situation* is applicable also, of course, to Celan's own country, and then to his adopted city, Paris (where, it

35. Jed Rasula, in "Encounters: American Poets on Paul Celan," *STCL* 8, no. 1
(Fall 1983): 115.
36. George Steiner, *After Babel: Aspects of Language and Translation* (Oxford,
1986), p. 389.
37. Peter Szondi, "Poetry of Constancy—Poetik der Beständigkeit: Celans
Übertragung von Shakespeares Sonett 105," in *Celan Studien,* pp. 13–45. Deleuze
and Guattari note that Kafka (who lived all of his life in Prague) pushed deterritorialization to the limit by adopting German "in its very poverty." German was
similarly already artificial for the Rumanian-born Celan, whose verse performs
even more extreme forms of pushing language to its limit.

should be added, he was never recognized as a writer of importance). Indeed, the *fausse situation* is the way in which "the Jew" is seen in general from within the minority discourse. Paul Celan inherits a false situation, a false site as the backdrop to what will become for him ever falser, muddier.[38]

Edmond Jabès calls writing "the suicidal effort to take on the word down to its last effacement where it stops being a word and is only the trace—the wound—we see of a fatal and common break: between God and man, between man and Creation."[39] If I have expatiated on the book for Celan, on the rehypostatization of the notion of the subject within the text, on the possibility of finding a speaking "I" with which to lament loss, it is because the context must be very clear in order to trace the extent of the wound, in Jabès's sense. The first wound for Celan, after he had chosen poetry, was Heidegger's silence in the face of the poet's question. The second was a charge of plagiarism, leveled seven years earlier than the meeting at Todtnauberg. These two events combined, I think, to annihilate the possibility of place—textual or geographic—for Celan. Indeed, the visit to Israel seems to have confirmed his conviction that place in both senses was unattainable for him; Celan killed himself less than a year after that trip.[40] On political and even metaphysical grounds, the minority discourse Celan espouses dooms his poetic-existential project from the start: as I have suggested, any textual "I" is already condemned to otherness. But the text gave Celan the illusion of a haven, and even a mission, until he was charged with plagiarism, the event to which we now turn.

In a 1960 letter to the editors of a journal, Claire Goll, widow

---

38. There is a way in which minority discourse itself insists on perpetrating the *fausse situation* into which the dominant discourse wants to place it.

39. Jabès, "The Key," in Hartman and Budick, *Midrash and Literature,* p. 356.

40. According to Yves Bonnefoy (personal communication, October 1988), the trip to Israel was a catastrophe because Celan felt so estranged there. Both the language and the country were beyond him, and Celan concluded that he should have moved there immediately after the war. Indeed, it was as if the possibility of becoming a majority, of losing his marginalized position, had become unthinkable to Celan. But there are other aspects of his estrangement: his attempt to understand the outer, physical landscape of Israel ("the Jew and nature are strangers to each other") as well as the inner was a struggle, as is obvious in his brief address to the Hebrew Writers' Association (*CP,* p. 57).

of the German Jewish refugee poet Yvan Goll, accused Paul Celan
of plagiarizing her husband's poetry.[41] Celan had visited the
couple in Paris, in October of 1949, shortly after his arrival in
France. Goll was sick; he died four months later. Celan asked the
dying man if he could translate his poetry, and Goll accepted the
offer, it seems. The couple even considered adopting the younger
poet, but the plan was abandoned after Goll's death. In any case,
Claire Goll complained that after her husband's death she saw
less and less of Celan—unless he needed money. She further
claimed that Celan's translations of Goll's poetry were so bad that
they were rejected by the Pflug publishing house in Zurich, to
which Celan had submitted them. Most of her letter reads like
that of a women who feels used and betrayed. And because Claire
Goll was alone, older, and bitter (not to mention a woman), her
letter is generally dismissed by Celan scholars (although not by
all, as we shall see). But there are, after all, concrete aspects to
the accusation.

In 1952, Richard Exner, the Germanist, heard Claire Goll give
a reading in California of her husband's verse. As Claire Goll reports it, he came up to her after her reading and asked her if she
was familiar with Celan's collection of verse, *Mohn und Gedächtnis*
(Poppy and remembrance). She was not, she said. Exner told her
that it contained lines utterly imitative of her husband's poem
"Traumkraut" (Dream weed). She adds that in 1955–56 Curt
Hohoff put the two poems in question side by side in an article,
demonstrating the "parallels." Frau Goll notes that two other critics can be added to the list of those who have openly accused
Celan of plagiarism or of "dependence" on Goll: Georg Maurer
and Kurt Pinthus.

Claire Goll's open letter fostered a spate of charges and coun-
tercharges. To Claire Goll, Maurer, Exner, and Pinthus was now
added Rainer Abels, whose article in *Die Welt* similarly claimed
certain "parallels" between Goll and Celan, with all of the worst
implications on Celan's side. In 1960, Reinhard Döhl came to Celan's rescue. In "Geschichte und Kritik eines Angriffs," Döhl ac-

---

41. Claire Goll, "Unbekanntes über Paul Celan," *Baubudenpoet* 5 (March–April
1960): 115–16.

cuses all the previous critics of unfairness and of bad philology. Döhl does careful biographical work and demonstrates, among other things, that Goll's widow was in fact familiar with the collection *Mohn und Gedächtnis* by 1949. Her story about Exner was a lie, at least on her side, although Exner is also implicated.[42] But in 1966 the most damaging accusation appeared: Erhard Schwandt's "corrections" of Döhl's article.[43] Goll's poem "Chant des invaincus" was written in French, and so published. But there was also a German version, the first and last stanzas of which read thus: "Schwarze Milch des Elends / Wir trinken dich / Auf dem Weg ins Schlachthaus / Milch der Finsternis" (Black milk of misery, we drink you on the way to the slaughterhouse, milk of darkness). And Celan: "Schwarze Milch der Frühe / wir trinken sie Abends . . ." (Black milk of early morning, we drink it in the evening . . .) Schwandt's article ends with a chronology of Goll and with thanks to his widow.

It seems safe to say that Schwandt won the day and that Döhl stood "corrected." Throughout the 1960s it was fashionable, in Germany, to assume that Celan had lifted from Goll, and from others as well. Not everyone shared this belief. But it is worth noting that the two literary prizes (the Bremen Prize and the Büchner Award) occurred just before the storm of accusations, and no other prize was to follow.

Celan was devastated. He wrote to Margul-Sperber of "the attempt to destroy me and my poems by a plagiarism campaign." Yves Bonnefoy remembers that, years after the accusation, he had spent the evening with his friend Celan: "[Celan] burst into sobs at the memory of a defamation he'd suffered some years before, a wound I thought time had healed."[44] Bonnefoy adds

42. Reinhard Döhl, "Geschichte und Kritik eines Angriffs: Zu den Behauptungen gegen Paul Celan," in *Deutsche Akademie für Sprache und Dichtung—Jahrbuch*, 1960–61, pp. 101–32.

43. Erhard Schwandt, "Korrekturen zum Bericht von Reinhard Döhl," in ibid., 1966, pp. 191–206.

44. Yves Bonnefoy, "Paul Celan," trans. Joel Golb, in "Translating Tradition: Paul Celan in France," special issue of *ACTS, a Journal of New Writing* 8/9 (1988): 9–14. Bonnefoy told me (personal communication, October 1988) that the events in Paris in May of 1968 added to the harm done Celan. Already burdened by manic-depressive illness, on lithium, which he complained destroyed his memory, Celan could hear the students protesting on the Boulevard Saint Michel. They were chanting "Nous sommes tous des Juifs allemands" (We are all German

that it was through him that Celan had met Goll in the first place, and says that while he himself stopped seeing "the sick, old man, himself an exile," Celan did not: "He never stopped offering care and affection—in order to see it all used against him later" (p. 12). Far from healing the wound, time had simply added to Celan's pessimism and despair. As Celan himself put it to Margul-Sperber, any attempt to put his poetry into question, as an accusation of plagiarism surely is, is equally an attempt to destroy him along with the poetry itself. While this is no doubt true of any "creative" writer, given the status of originality in this culture, it must have been doubly so for Celan, survivor and exile. The accusation of plagiarism plays several deadly games at the same time, but before we discuss these, we need first to return to the problem of the book.

                                        * *
                                         *

We have noted the peculiar relation, perceived by a number of contemporary Jewish writers, between the Jew and the Book: on the one hand, the book is the Jew's territory, the homeland in exile; on the other, no book can belong to an individual, since it is impossible to "own" words and since an idea is intangible and cannot therefore be property. Nevertheless, eighteenth-century rhetoric about manuscripts uses metaphors of landowning: keys, squatters, holdings, property, labor, occupancy, and so on are terms which abound. Thus the etymology of the term "author" is reinforced, as is the Lockean view that any labor (including "creative" labor in this case) belongs to the hand that produces it. These two views—that a book cannot be property, and that it is the fruit of labor—are clearly irreconcilable.

Mirroring this impasse is the famous argument between the booksellers and the copy makers in eighteenth-century England.[45] The booksellers argued perpetual right to an author for

---

Jews). This exploitation of the Holocaust, as Celan saw it, undertaken for reasons Celan considered trivial, seems to have acted as the final straw. He never left his apartment after that. Curiously, for Lyotard the sentence "Nous sommes tous des Juifs allemands" serves as one of the motivations for his book and his use of the term "les juifs" (see note 10 above).

45. We now have a repeat of the same debate, and of a very similar situation, with the law generated to protect videos from being pirated.

his work (not for high-minded reasons, but rather so that a book-seller could then buy those rights and own them in perpetuity). The copy makers, not surprisingly, argued that ideas could not be owned and that therefore "rights" of any kind were untenable. The Germans joined the debate: between 1773 and 1794 the problem of pirated copies spawned endless arguments about whether a book was a material or an ideal object. Fichte himself in 1793 wrote a piece called "Proof of the Illegality of Reprinting," which is important mainly for an entirely unrelated reason: the essay is one of the first to distinguish between the now belabored terms "form" and "content." [46] In the same year, in France, something astonishing occurred: on July 19, the National Convention passed a law on literary property which called itself a "declaration of the rights of genius." This law said that the originator of a work was the author, not God. Therefore the author had an "inviolable property right" to his work; it was a right and not a privilege granted by royal or divine decree.[47] The 1793 French law, most scholars agree, has given us the modern notion of "author," just as John Locke has given us the modern notion of personhood. As firmly as the modern definition of "author" may now be entrenched, however, its advent has in no way prevented debates concerning the individual rights of the author versus the common right to words and copying. Indeed, it has fueled such debates.

Throughout the eighteenth century both in England and on

46. For a superb historical explanation of this problem and its intricacies, see Mark Rose, "The Author as Proprietor: *Donaldson v. Becket* and the Genealogy of Modern Authorship," *Representations* 23 (Summer 1988): 51–85. I am indebted to Rose for this portion of my argument. See also Harry Ransom, *The First Copyright Statute: An Essay on "An Act for the Encouragement of Learning,"* 1710 (Austin, TX, 1956).

47. See M. J. Guillaume, ed., *Procès-verbaux du Comité d'Instruction Publique de la Convention Nationale* (Paris, 1894), 2: 80–82. For a history of French publishing, see Roger Chartier and Henri-Jean Martin, eds., *Histoire de l'édition française* (Paris, 1983–). Neither the law itself, nor the four-volume work cited here, takes female authorship into account. The term "author" means only male author. For an analysis of female writing in France, and of the broader theoretical issues raised by the history of female authorship, see Carla Hesse, "Reading Signatures: Female Authorship and Revolutionary Law in France, 1750–1850," *Eighteenth Century Studies* 22 (Spring 1989): 469–87. As Hesse points out, Gerard Genette is one of very few critics to discuss female authorship and to point to the need for further work in this area. See his *Seuils* (Paris, 1987).

the Continent, the argument rages: Is a book the private property of its author (and thus analogous to land), or is it a set of ideas, which have no bounds or marks whatever, nothing that is "capable of a visible possession," as one judge of the period phrased it?[48] Or, as Michel Foucault puts it in the much-read article "What is an Author?": "Since the eighteenth century, the author has played the role of the regulator of the fictive, a role quite characteristic of our era . . . of individualism and private property."[49]

These arguments and issues are all manifest in the making, changing, amending, or reversing of various copyright laws. The history of copyright law in the West functions like the semiology of changing notions of property, of the individual, of the author, and of creation itself. Moreover, it should be remembered that copyright, far from acting as a protection, is in fact a thinly veiled form of censorship. It is to censorship, far more than to freedom, that copyright is related. While the technical area of copyright law has (happily) been dealt with thoroughly by specialists, a few of its ramifications need to be mentioned here.[50]

In Anglo-Saxon law, the "subject" was invented early.[51] It has been argued that the intent of such a category as "person" was less the protection of the individual than an attempt to keep property from the peasants. Here Anglo-Saxon law parts ways with European law, which recognizes the rights of the individual in a different manner: the individual qua individual.

48. Justice Joseph Yates, in *Miller v. Taylor, English Reports,* 98:233. Cited also by Rose, "The Author as Proprietor," pp. 60–61.

49. Michel Foucault, "What Is an Author?" in *Textual Strategies: Perspectives in Post-Structuralist Criticism,* ed. Josue V. Harari (Ithaca, NY, 1979) pp. 141, 159. More recently, see Jack Stillinger, *Multiple Authorship and the Myth of Solitary Genius* (New York, 1991).

50. See especially Benjamin Kaplan, *An Unhurried Look at Copyright* (New York, 1967), for a thorough history of copyright in the West. See also J. C. T. Oates, *Cambridge University Library: A History from the Beginnings to the Copyright Act of Queen Ann* (New York, 1986); Lyman Rae Patterson, *Copyright in Historical Perspective* (Nashville, 1968); and Ransom, *The First Copyright Statute.* The latter includes the full text of the Act of 1710 and a calendar of events concerning literary property in England from 1476 to 1710.

51. For more on this issue, see *The Category of the Person,* ed. Carrithers, Collins, and Lukes (Cambridge, 1985). This collection of essays takes Marcel Mauss's work as a starting point. See in particular the essay by Arnaldo Momigliano, "Marcel Mauss and the Quest for the Person in Greek Biography and Autobiography," pp. 83–92, which argues that we can already recognize the modern notion of "person" in the biographies of Greek and Roman historians.

The first copyright act in the world, most experts agree, was England's Statute of Anne, 1709. The German states issued their first such laws ninety years later. On May 31, 1790, the first copyright law came into being in the United States, modeling itself on the Statute of Anne. Immediately problems arose, echoing the booksellers and the copyists of old: perpetual right became the issue, generating suits and countersuits. The question constantly raised is whether copyright is in itself a privilege or simply a description of property, whether it protects authors or profit. The U.S. Constitution professes to protect the author: "To promote the Progress of Science and Useful Arts, by securing for limited Times to Authors and Inventors the exclusive Right to their respective Writings and Discoveries" (Article I, section 8). "Authors and Inventors" are singled out for protection on the one hand, but society's rights are taken into consideration with "limited Times." [52] Thus the Constitution sees itself as balanced, looking out for both claimants.

Instantly, however, "limited Times" became a major issue. The Statute of Anne had given authors rights to their own books for fourteen years (then renewable). That was in 1710. Twenty years later, by which time it had been decreed that some books could be owned for twenty-one years, the situation was a thorough mess in England. The United States fared no better: the battle over how long an author could own the "work of his hands" raged fiercely. In 1906, the new Copyright Bill contemplated giving an author copyright for his lifetime plus fifty years thereafter. Several authors and musicians appeared before the Senate committee on December 6 of that year. One of them was Samuel Clemens, who clarified his view of the situation thus:

> I am aware that copyright must have a limit, because that is required by the Constitution of the United States, which sets aside the earlier Constitution, which we call the decalogue. The decalogue says you shall not take away from any man his profit. I don't like to be obliged to use the harsh term. What the decalogue really says is "Thou shalt not steal," but I am trying to use more polite language. [53]

52. William C. Warren in his introduction to Kaplan, *An Unhurried View of Copyright*, p. viii.
53. *Mark Twain's Speeches* (New York, 1910), p. 315.

Twain's humor amused the congressional audience, but did nothing to change the law in the way he and his colleagues wished.[54] Samuel Johnson's compromise is what has been generally adopted in Western copyright law: the author has rights during his lifetime plus a limited amount of time thereafter. This compromise, as Mark Rose notes, is a balance between the conflicting claims of the individual and of society.[55]

But Twain's remarks point to another problem, crucial to copyright law in particular and to any law attempting to mandate limits on creativity in general. The essence, or nature, of the book itself poses an intellectual problem, as we have discussed: Is it property (Twain at one point compared it to real estate, thus insisting upon the view that creative output is no different from any product of labor), or is it abstract, belonging to a community and thus to no particular individual? Because the status of the book as property is never fully decided upon, theft is always an issue in debates concerning the book's definition. Theft, in other words, is always the theme underlying any notion of originality; and paranoia is inevitable in this sense: it is impossible *not* to fear that your idea is being stolen by someone else. And this not only because, as with Freud, one may unconsciously sense that originality may be a myth; but also because it is unclear that what you are producing is yours to begin with, so that theft becomes a viable, condoned option. Thus plagiarism already partakes of the pathology of the Western notion "book," and the vocabulary and metaphors of theft abound.

For example, in 1853 a certain Judge Grier ruled that the German translation of *Uncle Tom's Cabin* did not infringe copyright law. A translation, he argued, is a "new book." He added that there can be "no hybrid between a thief and a thinker." In 1870, the U.S. law was amended to restrict translation. But now the line between an *idea*, presumably seen as transcending any particular language in which it is expressed, and always outside of copyright protection, and *form*, always with that protection, becomes very vague indeed. Thomas Mallon points out that "some-

54. For an exact description of the changes in the "new" copyright law of 1909, see Kaplan, *An Unhurried View of Copyright*, pp. 39–40.
55. Rose, "The Author as Proprietor," p. 59.

thing happened" in the seventeenth century which made copying (or imitation), until then an integral part of scholarship, reprehensible.[56] Classical literature makes imitation one of the cornerstones of education, a tradition continued in the Renaissance. "From Petrarch's sonnets to Milton's epics," declares one critic, "a major characteristic of Renaissance literature is the imitation of earlier texts."[57] According to Harold O. White, one of the first invectives against imitation took place in Italy in 1570, when one Lodovico Castelvetro wrote *Poetica d'Aristotele Vulgarizzata et Sposta:* "Castelvetro reverses every point of the classical theory of imitation, which he denounces as theft, and its practitioners (including Plautus, Terence, Seneca, Virgil, Boccaccio, Petrarch, and Ariosto) as thieves."[58] Although Castelvetro's views apparently had little immediate effect, they were increasingly to dominate the literary scene. Castelvetro gives an interesting reason for scorning imitators as "mere versifiers or translators only, notwithstanding that without merit of their own they have usurped the title of poet": for him, excellence depends upon the "labor" put out by the poet, and "whoever takes from another employs no labor in invention" (p. 26). Here we have an allusion, I think, to one of the major reasons for the scandal of plagiarism, or copying: that it does not entail much labor. As I will argue in a later chapter, the advent of the work ethic and the eventual appearance of Protestantism on the European scene may have combined to privilege labor to a point allowing for rigid judgments on plagiarism, copying, and other forms of what are considered to be easy means of fame (including, for example, loitering). In Castelvetro's early text we see a nascent hostility toward those who succeed without difficulty, those who enjoy too many fruits, as it were, of

56. Thomas Mallon, *Stolen Words: Forays into the Origins and Ravages of Plagiarism* (New York, 1989).

57. For an erudite and detailed discussion of imitation in the Renaissance, see Pigman, "Versions of Imitation in the Renaissance," 1–32. For imitation in classical texts, see Richard McKeon, "Literary Criticism and the Conception of Imitation in Antiquity," *Modern Philology* 34 (1936): 1–35. On the theory of imitation, see the excellent article by Thomas M. Greene, "Petrarch and the Humanist Hermeneutic," in *Italian Literature: Roots and Branches,* ed. Giose Rimanelli and Kenneth John Atchity (New Haven, 1976), pp. 201–24.

58. Harold O. White, *Plagiarism and Imitation during the English Renaissance: A Study in Critical Distinctions* (New York, 1965), p. 26.

too little labor. If there was no sweat on the brow in the undertaking, the result was unearned.

Kaplan, like Mallon, thinks that a sudden change in the view toward copying occurred at some point after the Renaissance. He explains this change by the weighty influence of Young, with his emphasis on original rather than imitative genius.[59] Arguably, by the eighteenth century Bacon's formula for scientific invention was being applied to literature, thus forcing an author into the position of being an inventor, with all of the "newness" and "originality" such a notion entails. It should be remembered that the U.S. Constitution speaks of "Authors and Inventors" in the same breath and, further, that it couples "Writings" with "Discoveries." So, to return for a moment to the previous chapter, Freud is not so odd in his insistence that his ideas were "discoveries." His use of a scientific, inventor's vocabulary is in keeping with a culture that applies the rules of scientific invention to literature. Freud, trained as a biologist, has no difficulty applying those principles to his frequently metapsychological texts.

Thus the notion of the "new" becomes tantamount to any claim of "authorship." New becomes opposed not so much to old as to unoriginal. Author, new, original, and spontaneous are the good words opposed to the bad: copyist, old, imitative (or stolen), and deliberate. Dr. Johnson, having wrestled with the difficulties of always having to come up with something new, concluded that there would never be such a problem for the good writer: "The complaint, therefore, that all topics are preoccupied, is nothing more than the murmur of ignorance or idleness, by which some discourage others and some themselves: the mutability of mankind will always furnish writers with new images, and the luxuriance of fancy may always embellish them with new decorations."[60] Nevertheless, argues Johnson, one must be careful before accusing an author of plagiarism—"not the most atrocious of literary crimes"—for the subject matter must be taken into consideration. There are certain topics (morality, history, "relations of social life") which have much in common, and one can-

59. Kaplan, *An Unhurried View of Copyright*, p. 24.
60. Samuel Johnson, *The Adventurer*, no. 99.

not therefore be surprised that texts on these matters bear "such a likeness as we find in the picture of the same person drawn in different periods of his life." The charge of plagiarism cannot therefore be "allowed with equal readiness" as the allegation of resemblance between authors. As one critic has recently remarked, "the definition of plagiarism is shaped less by clear ideas of right and wrong than by the particular, at times peculiar, character of the community in which the alleged offense takes place."[61]

A good example of how originality and, therefore, plagiarism, are governed more by the character of the community than by immutable notions of right and wrong is to be seen in the U.S. Copyright form. The wording of this form, fairly representative of most Western laws of this kind, suggests the warring claims between individual and community, between property and profit. The ostensible purpose of this particular form is to explain the new law, which was revised in 1978 for the first time since 1909. Here the problem of simple possession, as in land, is quickly ruled out: "Mere ownership of a book, manuscript, painting, or any other copy or phonorecord does not give the possessor copyright."[62] A book is not a holding, and so we are back to the booksellers' debate with the copyists. Moreover, if we look at what is and what is not protected, the warring factions are again evident. What is protected, according to the copyright form, are literary works, musical and dramatic works, pantomimes, motion pictures, and sound recordings. Also protected are choreographic, pictorial, sculptural, and dramatic works. But the form has a stern warning: "This list is illustrative and is not meant to exhaust the categories of copyrightable works. These categories should be viewed quite broadly so that, for example, computer programs and most 'compilations' are registrable as 'literary works'" (p. 4). What is *not* protected, however, is even more interesting: (1) works that are not written down; (2) titles, names, short

---

61. Jonathan Yardley, "Pirates of the Printed Page" (review of Mallon, *Stolen Words*), *Washington Post,* October 15, 1989.

62. *Circular R1: Copyright Basics.* This form is available from the Copyright Office, Library of Congress.

phrases, and slogans; and (3) "ideas, procedures, methods, systems, processes, concepts, principles, discoveries, or devices, as
distinguished from a description, explanation, or illustration."
The ground here is getting murky. Ideas and discoveries, the
givens of "originality," have no protection under U.S. copyright law.

The "author" is still "the person who actually created the
work," but the work itself has been relegated unabashedly and
unequivocally to the category of commodity: "Copyright protection subsists from the time the work is created in fixed form;
that is, it is an incident of the process of authorship. The copyright in the work of authorship *immediately* becomes the property of the author who created it." That sounds reassuring
enough; but there is a caveat: "Only the author or those deriv-
ing their rights through the author can rightfully claim copyright." What the prose contortions of this form demonstrate
(apart from the bureaucratic insistence upon obscurantism) is
that the notion of author, of property, and therefore of personhood, remains as destabilized as ever. Such a destabilization
is all the more evident in a document that assumes that all of
these notions are self-evident.

Plagiarism, as defined both etymologically and commonly, is
the theft of property by one individual from another, or, more
properly, a kidnapping—stealing something out of its proper context and putting it into a foreign one. But the property must be
tangible, must be "real estate"; hence the form's insistence that
only works which are written down can be protected.

* *
*

So was the widow Goll right about the most notorious of her
charges? That is, did the phrase "black milk" belong to her husband? The answer, of course, must be no. First, for a simple reason: even the American copyright form states that one cannot
protect "titles, names and short phrases." It is impossible to claim
the invention of so few words. Moreover, Goll's poem was published in New York in 1942, at a time (as Felstiner points out)
when Celan was in a Rumanian labor camp and "hardly likely to

have seen it."[63] Furthermore, Felstiner finds that the phrase exists in a poem by Rose Ausländer, a compatriot of Celan's. She uses the phrase "schwarze Milch" in a poem published in Czernowitz, Celan's birthplace. This poem, then, was no doubt familiar to Celan. But Ausländer said in 1972, upon being questioned, that she was honored by Celan's use of "her" phrase; thus she echoes Karl Kraus, who says in his paper on plagiarism that context is all.[64] Kraus argues that the same phrase in a different context is no longer the same phrase. There is also Immanuel Weissglass, another friend of Celan's, who wrote a similar poem. Finally, the image of black milk is *suggested* (not present, as Felstiner would have it) in Lamentations 4:7–8.

I would agree with many American critics (Felstiner in particular, but also Lyon and Golb) that the plagiarism affair was a convenient way for German critics to dismiss Celan as an important voice. Felstiner tells us that in the 1950s and 1960s, when Celan's work was very popular in Germany, the context (to return to Kraus's term) was vigorously apolitical and ambiguous; no mention was ever made of the fact that Celan was a Jewish poet who was a survivor of the Holocaust and who saw himself as a poet *of* the Holocaust. Even the avowed marginalization insisted upon in minority discourse is here unacknowledged. In the German texts in question (including textbooks), Celan was praised for his poetic form, the melodic tones of his verse, his innovations and neologisms, his debt to French Symbolism, to Rilke, to Hölderlin, and so on.[65]

It was not until the late 1960s that Celan became known in the United States, although he was known earlier than that to the poets of the Black Mountain School, as the poet Jerome Rothenberg (himself an early translator of Celan) reminds us.[66] In the United States, Celan is *the* Jewish poet of the Holocaust. The plagiarism accusation is very firmly and quickly dismissed:

63. John Felstiner, "Paul Celan's 'Todesfuge,'" in *Holocaust and Genocide Studies* 1, no. 2 (1986): 262, n. 26.
64. Karl Kraus, "Vom Plagiat," in *Die Sprache* (Munich, 1954), p. 149.
65. Felstiner, "Paul Celan's 'Todesfuge,'" p. 253.
66. Jerome Rothenberg, "Encounters: American Poets on Paul Celan," p. 110.

Felstiner, Lyon, Golb, to name just a few, regard it as an un-
founded claim made by an angry widow and taken up by anti-
Semites. It is clear that the rush to defend Celan here, and to
dismiss Claire Goll's charges, have as much to do with the response to the politics of anti-Semitism as does the insistence on
seeing him as a plagiarist or as an ahistorical poet. In Germany,
where he was first seen as a poetic voice in the nineteenth-
century tradition, the drive to accuse might be seen as a convenient way of expelling a poet whose growing international fame
was making it difficult, at best, to continue repressing the Holocaust in his work.

The rush to accuse and the rush to defend are both moves with
political agendas having little to do with Celan's poetic greatness
or, we might add, with whether he did in fact plagiarize (something which, quite apart from the legal ownership of two words,
will probably never be "proven" either way). What needs to be
taken into account, rather, is what such an accusation did to
Celan and, to return to the metaphor I have been using throughout this essay, on what grounds the charges rested. Within the
historical structure of Celan's European/Jewish context, within
his minority discourse, the charge of plagiarism holds a particular,
nefarious (if unacknowledged) power, which I have been trying
to bring out into the open.

To begin with, the stigma of plagiarism goes to the very heart
of any Western writer's "essence" (in the old Sartrean sense). Al-
exander Pope (who himself plagiarized) said that "the highest
praise of genius is original invention," and such a point of view
still prevails. For example, it seems difficult to assimilate the fact
that "Homer" was not an author in the modern sense of the word,
not even a scribe, but perhaps the best singer of that given tale
in the oral tradition from which it emerged. The literary canon
comprises not only works deemed to be great and important, but
also proper names which have come to resonate far beyond the
"person" they at least initially signified. Those proper names to
us "mean" originality.

What John Locke articulated in 1690 helped put firmly in
place the idea of personal property and thus of its ownership. In
Locke's words, whenever a man removes anything "out of the

state that Nature hath provided," and joins it with "something that is his own," he makes it his property. What we see here is the notion that original genius is tied to property, and property in turn to original genius and its products. Whoever first thought of the phrase "black milk" in this sense owns the phrase, since his or her self-definition as a writer depends precisely on such "something that is his own."[67]

But there is, too, the public realm, the *universitas*—that plurality of persons which also has rights and which makes for the polity. Here we are in the area of "common good," public domain, social consciousness, and so on. And here the phrase "black milk" cannot be protected; especially, ironically enough, once it becomes part of the public parlance. "Black milk" is now a cliché in German, and the poem "Todesfuge" appears in many German textbooks. So public, so common has the phrase become that many Germans can recite part of the poem without knowing that it comes from Paul Celan. We have come full circle: the dominant discourse has appropriated the minority discourse, which earlier sought to emulate the dominant one.

Celan described the plagiarism charge as "the attempt to destroy me and my poems." For what was the difference, finally, between himself and his poetry? Celan saw in the plagiarism campaign the symptoms of neo-Nazism and anti-Semitism in

---

67. See H. M. Paull, *Literary Ethics: A Study in the Growth of the Literary Conscience* (Port Washington, NY, 1928), which still provides a useful discussion of some of the issues inherent in "originality." The chapter on plagiarism fluctuates between caution ("A plagiarism is justified if it expresses an old thought in better language," p. 126) and stern reproof ("Every writer may do his best to avoid appropriating without acknowledgement the labor of others," p. 124). The book struggles courageously to distinguish between such terms as parody, plagiarism, piracy ("The plagiarist always hopes that he will not be found out whilst the pirate makes no secret of his crime," p. 45), forgery, ghostwriting, literary hoax, censorship, and so on. As such, Paull's study is a wonderful semiology of the hopelessness of disentangling plagiarism from its apparent opposite, originality. Most intriguing is Paull's discussion of a 1677 French work entitled *Le masque des orateurs* by a Sieur de Richesource (a perfectly invented name if ever there was one), which gives authors tools for disguising in their writing that of others. In a sort of Quintillian-cum-Longinus gone wrong, Richesource tells his followers to use such tricks as Elevation, Synonym, Multiplication, Opposition, Addition, Rejection, etc., to mask the original text. Paull includes an appendix with further details on Richesource's work (including the endless and hilarious full title).

postwar Germany. He had already developed a persecution complex, a paranoia, a political despair; the plagiarism charge exacerbated all of these. I think that his visit to Heidegger was tied to the plagiarism charge in this respect: if Heidegger could say even one word "from the heart," then perhaps the Book in both the common and the personal senses could be saved. But the philosopher remained silent, an outcome both inevitable and "logical" within the context we have been tracing. Heidegger's silence confirmed Celan's suspicion: the Book itself had become as suspect to Celan as his own books had become to his public. And with the Book gone, there was really nothing left for Celan.

"Yet every man has a property in his own person. This nobody has any right to but himself. The labor of his body, and the work of his hands, we may say, are properly his." These words have lost their meaning in light of the Holocaust. For Celan, the Holocaust erases his right to his own body, to his labor and the fruit thereof, to his rights as a "subject." The reconstruction of the subject (or of the memory of the subject) in the text was possible perhaps only because of Celan's belief in the Jew's special relation to the Book, as discussed at the beginning of this chapter. But it was also already impossible by virtue of the assumptions made by such a belief in the first place, by the discourse from which it springs. This is the double bind Celan lived, perhaps without knowing it. Both by the charge leveled against Celan of misrepresenting his own text, and by the silence of the "thinking man" called Heidegger, the man who more than any other was supposed to know of the "tear" (*Riss*) within the poet, the book itself became compromised ground for Celan. It no longer provided an exile from the exile, nor a place from which to speak. And so the subject, already at risk in the very grammar of "Todnauberg," already at odds with itself from within the discourse it saw as its own, was, very simply, occluded.

* *
*

The stigma of plagiarism is sometimes annihilated by the very myth of originality that produces it. The fact that Coleridge was a great literary thief is hardly mentioned in the enormous quantity of studies on that poet. Fruman's exhaustive work *Coleridge, the Damaged Archangel* is irrefutable; yet Coleridge's imago, so to speak, remains essentially unchanged.[68] One begins to wonder why one poet is vulnerable to such a charge while another is immune. Was Coleridge already too well established as the genius of the Romantics for any tarnishing of his image to be possible? Was Celan too easily dismissible: not yet established, writing of things most people would rather forget, pricking consciences that became angry in their guilt? When an author's name is equated with genius, literary decanonization seems unlikely, even in the face of proven plagiarism or forgery. There are, however, the exceptions discussed earlier: MacPherson, for example, and Chatterton. But such exceptions are far more the manipulation of the literary community and of criticism and its stakes than they are the symptoms of a concern for "authenticity," although authenticity is the ideology providing the terms of the exclusionary doctrine.

The next chapter will try to expand this point, and continue to probe the status of "genius" and originality as they relate to the problem of the subject and, in particular, to the female subject. We now turn to "Willy," the man who made creativity work in a different sense: he turned himself into his own product by fashioning himself into the figure of the genius-cum-man-about-town. It is "Willy" who sees how the notion of genius can be commodified; it is "Willy" who beats the literary establishment at its own game. Finally, it is "Willy" who achieves all of this fame on the backs of ghostwriters, the most talented of whom is his wife, "Colette."

68. Fruman, *Coleridge, the Damaged Archangel.* The argument continues to rage concerning the decanonization of Coleridge that Fruman's book undertakes. See the *Times Literary Supplement,* June–July 1989, for the testy exchanges between Fruman and defenders of Stephen Gill's biography of Wordsworth, which Fruman had reviewed critically (in *TLS,* May 5–11).

A P P E N D I X :

Todtnauberg

Arnika, Augentrost, der
Trunk aus dem Brunnen mit dem
Sternwürfel drauf,

in der
Hütte,

die in das Buch
—wessen Namen nahms auf
vor dem meinen?—,
die in dies Buch
geschriebene Zeile von
einer Hoffnung, heute,
auf eines Denkenden
kommendes
Wort
im Herzen,

Waldwasen, uneingeebnet,
Orchis und Orchis, einzeln,

Krudes, später, im Fahren,
deutlich,

der uns fährt, der Mensch,
der's mit anhört,

die halb-
beschrittenen Knüppel-
pfade im Hochmoor,

Feuchtes,
viel.

Arnica, eyebright, the
draft from the well with the
starred die above it,

in the
hut,

the line
—whose name did the book
register before mine?—,
the line inscribed
in that book about
a hope, today,
of a thinking man's

coming word
in the heart,

woodland sward, unlevelled,
orchid and orchid, single,

coarse stuff, later, clear
in passing,

he who drives us, the man,
who listens in,

the half-
trodden fascine
walks over the high moors,

dampness,
much.

—Translated by Michael Hamburger, *Poems of
Paul Celan* (New York: Persea Books, 1988),
p. 293. Reprinted by permission.

3

Disappropriating Colette

> You have curious things to eat,
> I am fed on proper meat;
> You must dwell beyond the foam,
> But I am safe and live at home.
>
> Little Indian, Sioux or Crow,
> Little frosty Eskimo,
> Little Turk or Japanee,
> O! don't you wish that you were me?
>
> —ROBERT LOUIS STEVENSON, "Foreign Children"

> Et chaque fois la lâcheté qui nous détourne de toute tâche
> difficile, de toute oeuvre importante, m'a conseillé de laisser
> cela, de boire mon thé en pensant simplement à mes ennuis
> d'aujourd'hui, à mes desirs de demain qui se laissent remâ-
> cher sans peine.
>
> —MARCEL PROUST, *Du côté de chez Swann*

LET US AGREE for a moment with several recent critics who
claim that one of the characteristics of modernism (which
we are obsessed with characterizing but seem unable to define, this inability in itself yet being another characteristic) is displacement. What some call "rootlessness," others (Guattari and
Deleuze, for example) call "deterritorialization." Other versions
include "the poetics of displacement" (Clifford), and such obvious
binary structures as inside/outside, center/margin, home/exile,
hegemony/minority, stable/nomadic—with the second term in
each case belonging to some facet of modernism.[1] These are no-

1. Guattari and Deleuze: see, e.g., chap. 2, n. 11, above. Clifford: see chap. 2,
no. 18, above.

tions linking "modernism" to minorism, and have to do with writers who for one reason or another have been geographically exiled; refugees who have a notion of "home" even if a "reterritorialization" is but a necessary fiction, and even if the place of "origin" is no less an invention. Marginalizations of the sort Guattari and Deleuze talk about, whether based on racism, xenophobia, religious intolerance, or other such bigotries, insist upon a certain fiction of origin, a certain idea of "home" and of who belongs there, and hence on a certain concomitant notion of "purity." And such a fiction is in place, I would argue, even in books that overtly reject origin as a site, claiming (as does Clifford, for example) that modernity is rootlessness, what he calls "translation and transplanting." But these metaphors are already origin-sited, of course. Both translation and transplanting assume a home (text in the first case and ground in the second).

Few of these studies on deterritorialization, however, consider the matter from a gendered perspective; a perspective that raises different issues within what is apparently the same perimeter. Clearly, to give but one example, "home" is a very curious notion for women—it is frequently as much an exile as is an adopted country, or "host," for a refugee.[2] It is often experienced as a prison, not a refuge. As Simone de Beauvoir notes somewhere in *The Second Sex,* one reason women have failed to band together is their isolation, along precisely the lines making for more hegemonic types of exclusion: class, race, national identity, religion. To these we might add the more gender-specific (that is, woman-oriented) exclusions, or divisions, created by the dominant culture: age, sexual practices, physical appearance, and marital status. Far from being the fortress that protects them against the world, "home" for women is often just a fortress—exclusionary in its own way for reasons having to do with the hegemony's

2. One of the few critics who make this point is Caren Kaplan, who also cites the American writer Minnie Bruce Pratt's point that "being homesick while 'at home' is worse than moving away from home." See Caren Kaplan, "Deterritorializations: The Rewriting of Home and Exile in Western Feminist Discourse," in *Cultural Critique,* no. 6 (see chap. 2, n. 12, above). These instances of gendered deterritorializations also include the problems of "home" as posed by a homophobic culture.

perpetration of sexual competition and social maiming.[3] I am referring here to Western women, and largely first-world women at that. But that is Colette's context, whose story is part of what is at issue here.

The questions to be raised at this point are: What is deterritorialization for a woman writer?[4] Is it possible to be deterritorialized in the first place when there has never been a place, or even the fiction of a place, where you were at home? For despite the private space called "home" that a woman frequently creates for others, she is not "at home" anywhere in the world, in the public sphere. Thus home itself, that so-called private space, is often more a confinement than refuge.[5] In terms of everyday life, a white, bourgeois woman in late nineteenth-century France creates a domestic rather than a social space. It is a space created for others, and one in which she is frequently the only stranger. Can there be a "reterritorialization" within such a context?

And yet, as Henri Lefebvre has suggested, in many ways everyday life is a spatial concept that refuses the usual binary of subject/object but, rather, includes both.[6] Indeed, the very terms "public" and "private" are in themselves largely gendered; everydayness in Lefebvre's sense may help undercut such binary oppo-

3. Many more recent formulations of this problem articulate the essentialist versus "difference" positions, as they are now referred to in current parlance. See, for example, Chandra Mohanty, "Under Western Eyes: Feminist Scholarship and Colonial Discourse," *Feminist Review*, no. 30 (Autumn 1988): 61–88. Mohanty discusses the obvious dangers of an essentialist view which sees women as homogenous and "identifiable prior to the process of analysis" and, in particular, sees the notion of "Third World women" as the production of (feminist) Western texts. But she is also clear, as was Beauvoir, in arguing for "the urgent political necessity of forming strategic coalitions across class, race and national boundaries" (61–62 ff.). Beauvoir's point was that it was in the hegemonic culture's interest to maintain the isolation of woman from woman, and thus to make such coalitions nearly impossible. As Gayatri Spivak notes, essentialism can be a powerful weapon in the hands of the dispossessed.

4. By "woman writer" here I mean a white, first-world woman who writes at the end of nineteenth-century France—a woman such as Colette.

5. On the problem of home as prison, see for example Nina Auerbach, *Romantic Imprisonment* (Ithaca, NY, 1987). See also Ellen Nerenberg's doctoral dissertation, "Habeas Corpus: The Gendered Subject in Prison," especially the chapter "House Arrest" (University of Chicago, forthcoming). See also Donna Haraway on "home" in *Primate Visions: Gender, Race, and Nature in the World of Modern Science* (New York and London, 1989) p. 329.

6. See for example, Henri Lefebvre, *Critique de la vie quotidienne* (Paris: L'Arche, 1958–81), 3 vols.

sitions, such stereotyped notions of, for example, domestic space as against "the world," or the political as against "the private." As almost any situation makes clear, domestic space cannot refuse elements of the world, and the private is never apolitical.[7]

Moreover, the world and the political intrude a priori into the situation of the woman writer: the question of ownership and possession is inevitably raised. Can female ownership of any kind be possible in terms that the dominant culture (here patriarchal and male, obviously) will agree to recognize, given that it perpetrates a structure granting women neither first nor even fictional (not to mention biblical) "originary" status? What does it mean to seek recognition, as Colette did, from the very culture that makes such a seeking doomed to fail?

Given that women do not have the status of "person" in the sense that John Locke (who certainly was not including women in his *Treatises*) articulates it, they cannot *expect* to "have a property in their own person," or, as it logically follows, to own the labor of their bodies (continuing Locke's phrasing) or the work of their hands.[8] Thus, originality and its risks, as I have been formulating them, cannot be the central and motivating myth for a Colette that it is for the men we have considered (Descartes,

7. As Chantal Mouffe and Ernesto Laclau, among many others, point out, a fixed line cannot be drawn between public and private. For Mouffe and Laclau, the subject is surrounded by a multitude of discourses which force the politicization of the private (and vice versa). The struggle of women is one of several which, beginning in the nineteenth century, led to the destabilization of the public/private binary. See *Hegemony and Socialist Strategy: Towards a Radical Democratic Politics* (London and New York, 1985). Among those who have written extensively on the place of the private as against the social are Hannah Arendt, *The Human Condition* (Chicago, 1970); Jürgen Habermas, *Structural Transformation of the Public Sphere*, trans. Thomas Burger (Cambridge, MA, 1989); and Walter Benjamin—e.g., "Louis Philippe of the Interior," in *Reflections*, ed. Peter Demetz, trans. Edmund Jephcott (New York, 1986), not to mention Benjamin's entire *Arcades* project. More recently there has been the enormous (and problematic) *A History of Private Life* in five volumes planned by the late Philippe Ariès and translated by Arthur Goldhammer (Cambridge, MA, 1992).

8. For Locke, women gave up their civil rights when they agreed to marry. See S. M. Okin, *Women in Western Political Thought* (Princeton, 1992) for a discussion of Locke's views on women's rights. See also Catherine Hall, "Private Persons versus Public Someones: Class, Gender and Politics in England, 1780–1850," in *Language, Gender and Childhood*, ed. C. Steedman, C. Urwin, and V. Walderdine (London, Boston, and Henley, 1985), pp. 10–33. Hall argues that women were marginalized with respect to public and therefore political life because "they did not possess the necessary prerequisites for citizenship" (p. 30).

Freud, Celan). The dominant culture, which defines women's exclusion, simultaneously provides the logic by which all attempts
to see woman as person, owner of her body and labor, must be
seen as intrinsically nonsensical. Originality is not a woman's issue since, within the terms defining her, origin and a space of
grounding are unimaginable. In this sense we might ironically
note that for those who claim rootlessness and lack of site of origin to be the primary principles of modernism, "woman" ought
to be the best example. Indeed, as we shall later have occasion to
suggest, it may be for this reason rather than for the more overt
ones that modernism is often regarded as "feminized."[9]

Earlier we discussed Michel de Certeau's articulation of the notion of place in history. Let us examine another passage from Certeau's *The Writing of History,* considering it from the position of
woman:

> Writing is born of and treats of admitted doubt, of explicit division;
> in sum, of the impossibility of its own place. It articulates the con-
> stantly initial fact that the subject is *never authorized* by a place, that
> he could never be founded on an inalterable *cogito,* that he is al-
> ways foreign to himself and forever deprived of an ontological
> ground, and hence is always *left over, superfluous,* always the *debtor
> of a death,* indebted in respect to the disappearance of a genealogi-
> cal and territorial "substance," and bound to a name lacking
> property.[10]

I use Certeau as only one of many possible examples to underscore the fact that much of what calls itself Western metaphysics
is currently engaged in reminding the subject of *his* inauthentic-
ity, lack of sovereignty, instability. The statement "The subject is
never authorized by a place" has a particular resonance with the
situation of Paul Celan. "He is always foreign to himself"—he is
always deterritorialized already, and must be made conscious of

9. But it is equally often considered "virilized." Obviously, notions of what
is feminized and masculinized (or virilized, as I clumsily have put it) are often
problematic, not to say essentialist, in themselves. I therefore use these terms
with caution and with frequent scare quotes. The gender of modernism will be
an issue in chapter 4.

10. Michel de Certeau, *The Writing of History,* trans. Tom Conley (New York,
1988), p. 320; emphasis Certeau's. In this work, at the end of his discussion of
Freud, Certeau himself continues the theme of the Wandering Jew and his lack
of place (*non lieu*).

this state lest he take his utterances and writings as grounding. But these warnings, which remind the subject of his nostalgia for a unified, seamless point of origin, and of his lack of ontological ground, are meaningless if addressed to the female subject. It is in this context that I bring the Certeau passage into the discussion: the stakes of the Western subject are blatantly male; but we cannot ignore the extent to which its parameters and the questions which arise from them are inapplicable to the experience and ontology of first-world women. It is only by juxtaposing the female "situation" with the male metaphysical text that the presuppositions of the latter become absurd with respect to the former.

The absurdity is intensified with the particular situation of the woman writer. As Andreas Huyssen has put it, "given the fundamentally differing social and psychological constitution and validation of male and female subjectivity in modern bourgeois society, the difficulty of saying 'I' must of necessity be different for a woman writer . . . The male, after all, can easily deny his own subjectivity for the benefit of a higher aesthetic goal, as long as he can take it for granted on an experiential level in everyday life."[11] By remaining within the rules and structures of hegemonic culture, one is not only defined by it, as is clearly the case for women; one is also put in the position of answering its questions rather than being able to ask it questions of one's own. As a writer, Colette tried to play by the rules, but she was, of course, constituted by the very rules she was trying to bend (I do not even say break). Again, let us juxtapose Certeau's metaphysical assertion that the subject is "linked to a name that cannot be owned" with Colette's experiential level: legally, she lost every battle concerning publishing rights that she waged in her "own" name.

There are already two contradictions for Colette, or for any woman writing in fin de siècle France, in the previous assertion. To being with, women had no legal rights. The husband of a successful writer of the period, upon informing his appalled wife that

11. Andreas Huyssen, *After the Great Divide: Modernism, Mass Culture, Postmodernism* (Bloomington, IN, 1986), p. 46.

he intended to sign her books with his name, explained: "The law authorizes it . . . The work of a wife belongs to her husband."[12] This is simply a reiteration of the previous point that in Lockean terms women own neither their bodies nor the labor of their hands and consequently are not persons. Conversely, being a priori not persons, women cannot own the fruits of their labor.

The second contradiction in the earlier assertion is that a woman writer frequently does not own her name either, or does not even have a name of her own. The secondariness (or derivativeness, lack of origination), of the name for a woman writer in this context mirrors the secondary ontological status that women receive metaphysically, legally, and so on.[13] "Colette" is in fact the father's family name (the author's "maiden name"); it will become a pen name chosen for the writer by her husband.[14]

Originality is the issue that keeps resurfacing for the writer Co-

12. Cited by Carla A. Hesse, in "Reading Signatures: Female Authorship and Revolutionary Law in France, 1750–1850," *Eighteenth Century Studies* 22 (Spring 1989): 469–87.

13. It should not be forgotten that until 1965 a married woman in France could not publish a text or engage in any form of work without permission from her husband. The law of February 10, 1938, gave women full civil rights (*le plein exercice de sa capacité civile*), including the right to open a bank account, sign and receive checks, inherit property, own and distribute private property. But the same article of that law, no. 215, which grants women civil rights, also has a major caveat: the woman's rights are restricted according to the laws governing the kind of marriage she has (separation or not of property). Since most women married under the law of communal property, the 1938 law did little to help them. A 1907 law had allowed women to work for their own salaries, but since this right was reiterated in the 1938 law, it had obviously remained an issue. The latter law remains contested as well, for there is a 1963 law that specifically (again) allows women to open their own bank accounts, and a 1965 law that revises (and improves upon, which for women is not saying much) the Napoleonic Code, reiterating the right of women to work without their husband's permission. At the same time, there has been the 1945 law granting women the vote, and a 1946 equal rights clause to the French constitution. All of which shows that the rights of women have been continually contested during the century that purports to "grant" them equality. For a useful overview of this willed legal confusion, see Maite Albistur and Daniel Armogathe, *Histoire du féminisme français* (Paris, 1977), pp. 438 ff.

14. The extent of the complexity of this matter concerning female signature in general and "Colette" in particular can be judged from the number of critics who talk about how Colette was finally able to sign her "own name" after the escape from her husband. On the problem of naming in Colette, see Michèle Blin Sarde, "The First Steps in a Writer's Career," in *Colette, the Woman, the Writer,* ed. Erica M. Eisinger and Mari McCarthy (University Park, PA, 1981), pp. 16–21. See also Susan D. Cohen, "An Onomastic Double Bind: Colette's *Gigi* and the Politics of Naming," *PMLA* 100, no. 5 (1985): 793–809. Finally, see Colette's *Mes Apprentis-*

lette; but origin itself is already at stake in the very mythology surrounding her arrival, her "birth" (to continue the metaphors of origin), into the literature scene. About one fact, however, there is no argument: when Gabrielle Sidonie Colette discovered that her husband of a few months was having an affair, she was devastated. She hid her misery from her mother, "Sido," in order to protect her from knowing of her unhappiness, and also because Sido had told her not to marry in the first place. Isolated in a dirty, drafty Paris apartment, lonely and very young, far from Sido and her beloved countryside, Gabri fell ill and nearly died. The doctor's diagnosis: loss of the will to live. The indomitable Sido arrived in Paris to nurse her daughter back to health, and, as we know, she succeeded.

Here we arrive at the various myths of the writer's origin. All the narratives of the writer's inception or "birth" see the husband as the "father" of the writer who was to become Colette. The writer herself, in other words, is not viewed as the origin of her own writing or, indeed, of her own existence as writer. It should be remembered, too, that the young Gabri was marginalized by more than her sex: she was a country girl in the *métropole;* she had a Burgundian accent and rolled her r's, much to the amusement of the Parisians; she was a bourgeoise in Willy's flamboyantly bohemian world; she was a nature lover exiled in a large city; and, of course, she was a woman undertaking a largely male profession. As Claude Mauriac puts it, she was at the margins of herself as well as of society.[15]

One version of her literary inception has the guilty husband suggesting to Gabri that she distract herself during her convalescence by writing her memoirs. As most other versions would have it, however, and as the writer herself was later to tell it, her husband needed money. He was constantly seeing the wolf at the door; according to him, they were always broke. So, in the winter

---

sages (Paris, 1936), on the origins of her *nom de plume*. Most of my biographical account is based on this work and on Willy's own autobiographical work, in a limited *pro amicis* edition, *Indiscretions et commentaires sur les "Claudine"* (Paris, 1962).

15. ". . . en marge de la société, mais aussi en marge d'elle-même." In *Colette par Colette* (Paris, 1976), p. 331. Colette also had "black blood," a fact frequently cited to "explain" her curly hair and "exotic" face.

of 1895, he told her that funds were low and suggested that she write a titillating version of her school years.

Gabri dutifully went out, bought notebooks like those she used when she was a schoolgirl, and began to write. Her husband read the result and declared it to be no good ("I was wrong, there's nothing in it"). She was relieved and went back to her jealousy-ridden, lonely days centered on her cat, couch, and reading.[16] Two years later, her master (as she sometimes referred to her husband) cleaned out his desk and found the notebooks, which he thought he had discarded. He reread them and declared himself to have been an idiot ("Je ne suis qu'un con"). He took them to a publisher, who refused the work, and then to a second, who did the same. Finally, the book was accepted by Ollendorf. *Claudine à l'école* appeared in 1900, signed by the husband under the best known of the many names he invented for himself, "Willy." He had not yet decided on the name "Colette" for his wife, a name in any case unnecessary at that point since only his name appeared on the title page.

"And that," Colette was to write much later, "is how I became a writer." Geneviève Dormann puts it more directly: "Ultimately, we ought to be grateful to Willy. He gave us Colette. He not only made her write: he taught her how to write."[17] Sido herself, who had always disliked Willy, wrote to her daughter in 1911: "I often say to myself what you acknowledge to yourself, however vaguely: that if you had not spent some time with that character, your talent would never have been revealed."[18] Clearly, Willy provided the impetus for Colette's discovery of writing.

When Willy realized that his wife had real talent, he locked her up for four hours a day and forced her to produce pages filled with writing. Dormann sees this incarceration as "a boon for the feminists" (one wonders what her relation to "the feminists" is).[19]

---

16. "Delivrée, je retournai au divan, à la chatte, aux livres, au silence, à une vie que je tâchais de me rendre douce, et dont j'ignorais qu'elle me fut malsaine." *Oeuvres* (Pléiade ed., Paris, 1984), p. 1240.

17. Geneviève Dormann, *Colette: A Passion for Life* (New York: Abbeville Press, 1985), p. 45.

18. In the personal collection of Bertrand de Jouvenal. Letter of February 4, 1911.

19. The French reads: "Colette, enfermée par son mari pour qu'elle écrive, quel nanan pour les féministes qui, plus tard, tenteront de la récuperer à leur

Indeed, critics break down into two camps on this situation: the "feminist" (*sic*) view, which sees Colette as the victim of a slave-driving husband who was obsessed with money; and the friends of Willy, and/or the nonfeminists, who see Willy as the creator or, at the very least, facilitator of Colette.

My purpose here is not to establish (as if that were possible) how much of Colette "belongs" to Willy, nor to subscribe to either camp. Rather, I am concerned with the insistence upon the originality myth in connection with the term "author," a myth that is at stake in all of these defenses or accusations. Indignant statements to the effect that Willy certainly had nothing to do with Colette's beginnings are no different at this level than those which announce that, without Willy, Colette the writer would not have existed. In other words, the unspoken question raised in these studies is where to situate originality, and thus how to assess Colette in the canon. Putting Colette's originality at stake is a gesture toward determining her importance as a writer and her place in the hierarchy. But what is never put into question is the assumption that the sole right and function of literary criticism is to make and uphold the verity of these judgments and to recognize whether what seems to be originality is in fact bogus or genuine. Moreover, the very notion "originality," as I have previously stated, is on an epistemological level a male, phallocentric metaphor (and remains so, whether used by a male or a female critic). The implications, for a woman writer, of an apparently objective assessment of her relation to originality, and thus her place in the canon, should be evident.

It is therefore worth looking more closely at a few more of these interpretations of Colette's beginnings as a writer, in order to see how the reliance on originality plays itself out in what purports to be judicious literary criticism, how much the notion of "authenticity" dominates those judgments, and how much it is, finally, in the interests of literary criticism itself to maintain the (gendered) originality myth it professes merely to interpret.

Most biographers and friends of both Colette and Willy agree

---

usage, comme elles le feront pour George Sand et pour toutes les femmes exceptionnelles, en les transformant en victimes de mâles implacables." Geneviève Dormann, *Amoureuse Colette* (Paris, 1985), p. 40.

that Willy was in some central way responsible for bringing Colette to the act of writing, even if, like one critic, they insist that "Willy was an accident, Sido was necessary."[20] The other extreme is a critic who says, without intended irony, that "The *Claudines* owe a great deal to Colette," but that Willy's is the major voice.[21] Yet another simply refers to "Willy, author of the *Claudines*."[22]

"Never had an author felt less of a vocation," one biographer notes in 1983; "Willy had driven her to her career."[23] Another biographer, in 1974, referring to Colette's daily imprisonment, serenely comments, "Colette did not really object. Having no literary ambition for herself, she seems to have been rather amused by the whole affair."[24] John Updike, in a 1980 review of Colette's letters in English translation, claims: "Without Willy, there would have been no Colette."[25]

Claude Farrère, a friend of Colette's, wrote to his own friend Richard Anacréon concerning this birth of a writer and her debt to her husband: "Colette was a wild foal. Willy was a trainer and he taught her to win by humiliating her. Could she have won the Grand Prix on her own? I am far from convinced. And even if she had done it by herself, it would have taken twenty years instead of two."[26] Why would it have taken Colette ten times longer to become a writer without Willy? Farrère continues, "She would never have succeeded because she is very lazy and hates writing."

Here we encounter the curious issue of laziness, which will become a primary concern in this and in the following chapter. For now, however, I wish only to comment that in the account

20. Jane Lilienfeld, "The Magic Spinning Wheel . . . ," in *Mothering the Mind: Twelve Studies of Writers and their Silent Partners,* ed. Ruth Perry and Martine W. Brownley (New York, 1984), p. 176.

21. Pierre-Robert Leclerc, "Le Moi-je de Colette, ou l'affirmation d'une écriture féminine," *Etudes* 14 (June 1986): 786.

22. *"Belles Saisons": A Colette Scrapbook,* assembled and with a commentary by Robert Phelps (New York, 1978), p. 51 (caption to a photograph of Willy).

23. Joanna Richardson, *Colette* (New York, 1983), p. 28.

24. Robert D. Cottrell, *Colette* (New York, 1974), p. 28.

25. John Updike, *The New Yorker,* December 29, 1980.

26. Claude Farrère, cited by Dormann, *Colette: A Passion for Life,* p. 45.

by Farrère, who saw himself as a friend of Colette's, the meta-phors have not so subtly shifted. From Sido's admission that thanks to Willy, Colette's talent was revealed, we come to the taming of the wild animal by humiliation. There is the concomi-tant view that Willy did the work (like a good trainer), "breaking" the foal Colette into liking writing, and vanquishing her laziness. The agency, in other words, is his. "Ah!" Willy remarks at some point, "if only she weren't so lazy." Recall that in the other re-marks just cited by critics, Colette is described as lacking discipline and ambition—two major elements in "laziness."

The laziness motif keeps reappearing. Even in Elaine Marks's pathbreaking book on Colette, written in 1960 and remarkable for the feminist slant it takes well before such interpretations be-came almost standard, we read: "And yet it is quite possible that at first Colette was lazy, at least with regard to writing."[27] Not that there isn't, as Kristin Ross reminds us, a "right to laziness."[28] What is curious about the application of the word "lazy" in Co-lette's case is that it is always with reference to her initial reluc-tance to write, and therefore necessarily connected with her "originality."

Yet the avoidance of writing, and the apparently contradictory obsession with writing itself (talking about it, promising to do it, pretending to do it, being blocked, and so on), describes not Co-lette but the two most important men in her life at the time of the *Claudines:* her husband and her father. It is Colette, in fact, who demystifies the act of writing by noting wryly that there is no more merit to writing than to making shoes. For her, in other words, writing is a trade, a work of the hand, not an activity to be romanticized. "No," she says in *Journal à rebours*, "I don't know how to write. In my youth, I never, *never* wanted to write." To the Belgian Literary Academy, on the occasion of her inauguration in 1936, she said, "I became a writer without realizing what was

27. Elaine Marks, *Colette* (New Brunswick, NJ, 1960), p. 30.
28. Kristin Ross, *The Emergence of Social Space: Rimbaud and the Paris Commune,* Theory and History of Literature, vol. 60 (Minneapolis, 1988), pp. 47–74. The phrase "the right to laziness" is taken from Paul Laforgue's *Le Droit à la paresse* (1880). The issues raised here concerning work and leisure will be taken up again in chapter 4.

happening." And yet it becomes an obsession: "I still don't know when I shall succeed in not writing."[29]

Colette's father, on the other hand, was always mysteriously talking of his writing (and he did write the occasional ditty or poem). When he died, his children found boxes filled with large, bound volumes, all of them bearing titles, and all of them with blank pages. "Hundreds and hundreds of blank pages," writes Colette, "imaginary works, mirage of a writer's career" (ibid., p. 8). Laziness, however, is never mentioned in connection with the father. Indeed, Colette, whose pen name is his, is strangely haunted by the father who was obsessed with writing and could not write: "It was he," she claims, "who was trying to come to the surface and live again when I began obscurely to write" (ibid.). With the paralyzed father as a type of inverted muse, Colette will write more and more to overcome the blankness of the page.[30]

Willy himself had a horror of the blank page, and was pathologically unable to write. Michèle Sarde notes: "The exceptional thing about Willy was that he never wrote so much as a word himself, aside from telegrams, oceans of letters, a few pun-filled poems, some few articles he may possibly have actually authored—and, of course, his famous account book."[31] It is Colette who says that Willy's letters demonstrate "the refusal to write." But whereas Jules Colette had pretended to write, hiding what Sarde calls his "literary impotence" from his family, Willy chose the path of employing ghostwriters. These writers, *nègres* ("niggers," which, as Sarde puts it, is "unfortunately"—and I would add, not coincidentally—the French term), wrote works that Willy signed. One of these *nègres* was of course Colette herself.

29. Cited by Françoise Mallet-Joris, "A Womanly Vocation," in Eisinger and McCarthy, *Colette,* p. 14.

30. On the father's influence upon the daughter's writing, see Jerry Aline Flieger, "Colette and the Captain, Daughter as Ghostwriter," in *Refiguring the Father: New Feminist Readings of Patriarchy,* ed. Patricia Yaeger and Beth Kowaleski-Wallace (Carbondale, IL, 1989), pp. 22–38. The pages of the Captain's book were not entirely blank: there was, as Colette tells us, "the page that bore the dedication: TO MY DEAR SOUL, HER FAITHFUL HUSBAND: JULES-JOSEPH COLETTE." Sido's house is as if haunted by this embarrassment of white pages, which are never used up in spite of Sido's attempts to make good use of them after the father's death (Flieger, p. 26).

31. Michèle Blin Sarde, *Colette: A Biography,* trans. Richard Miller (New York, 1980), p. 138.

When he was dealing with his wife, Willy's "horror" of the blank page translated into an insistence for pages covered in ink: "Show me your papers," Willy would say to his wife after having locked her in her room for the requisite four hours. "What I was forced to show," she writes in *Mes apprentissages,* "were blackened pages." And she adds, "I admit that such details of my daily incarceration are not greatly to my credit." [32]

Equally to the point, however, is the fact that Willy's horror of the blank page is consciously tied to that of Mallarmé (who knew and admired Willy). In these gentlemen, such a horror is an intriguing neurosis; in Colette, however, her initial distaste for the empty pages confronting her, and what she called, in a parody of Mallarmé, *l'angoisse de la page bleue* ("the anxiety of the blue page"—Colette's favorite writing paper was blue) is "laziness." Clearly, laziness here is gendered. [33]

The assumption that Colette, unlike her father or the "tireless" (as he is frequently described) Willy, was lazy because she disliked writing extends itself in odd ways. Dormann, for example, reminds us in her biography that many people lock up their spouses to force them to write. Anatole France's friend "the strict Madame Arman de Caillavet," for example, played the role of jailer (Dormann omits to say, however, that Caillavet did not sign her name to France's books). Dormann's conclusion is extraordinary: "The work of a writer is often so painful that we know several today who would not be unhappy if a familiar hand occasionally became a forceful one." [34] This is a fairly complicated statement which has, once again, to do with the mythologies of writing (and not with Dormann herself or with her vaguely irritating biogra-

32. *Colette par Colette* (Paris, 1976), p. 386.
33. There are times when Willy is accused of a certain "indolence." Marks (in *Colette*), for example, cites J. H. Rosny-Aîné as saying that Willy had "a wealth of knowledge which his indolence never allowed him to deepen" (p. 30). The indolence in question (which is here not identical to laziness) has more to do with dilettantism than with the task of writing—a task that Willy in any case never undertook.
34. My translation. "La mise au travail d'un écrivain est, souvent, si pénible que nous en connaissons quelques-uns, aujourd'hui, qui ne seraient pas mécontents si une main familière se faisait, parfois, contraignante." Dormann, *Amoureuse Colette,* p. 41. Interestingly, the American illustrated edition of the work tones down the bizarreness of this statement. That translation reads: "Writers often have great difficulty in getting down to work and one can think of several modern

phy). To begin with, it says the same thing as the Farrère letter: writers are undisciplined and need to be tamed; they don't know what is in their own best interest, so that what may seem to be humiliation and force are in fact tactics undertaken for the writer's own good. Thus the relation of a writer to his or her spouse or lover should be sado-masochistic in many instances if the writer is to succeed. The nonwriter in this partnership, in other words, is being selfless and loving. Such a view displaces agency onto the jailer. The writer is seen much as Freud (who inherits his own views from the early German romantics) views the artist in general: neurotic, paralyzed, unable to function (significantly enough) in the everyday world, and utterly lacking in any sort of sense, common or other. But, after all, the person of genius has frequently been imagined, since the romantics, as an *idiot savant*.[35]

In a doubly bizarre move, the Dormann statement mirrors the displacement of agency with the metaphor of the "familiar hand" (*une main familière*), which belongs, not to the writer, as one would assume (the hand, after all, is the usual metaphor for handwriting, and in French for signature), but to the jailer whose (affectionate) hand has become forceful.[36] Writing, let us not forget, does partake of labor; writing is the work of the hand, and writing implements are its tools. But the statement by Dormann insists upon the romantic genius version of writing; the writing-as-labor is elided, its very labor displaced by a flick, as it were, of the hand metaphor. It is the jailer who does the "work" so that the genius can simply "be."

Willy's genius lay in making use of both aspects of writing: on the one hand, he exploited the public's mystique of the original

---

authors who might welcome occasional friendly pressure to make them write." *Colette: a Passion for Life,* trans. David Macey (New York, 1985), p. 45. To describe what Willy did to Colette to make her write as "friendly pressure" is a wonderful howler.

35. See, for Freud's views on the artist, for example, *Leonardo da Vinci and a Memory of His Childhood* (1910).

36. Colette herself uses the metaphor of the hand in this context: she speaks specifically about the hand (Willy's) which turned the key to her cell: "Peace upon that hand, then, now dead, which did not hesitate to turn the key in the lock." Significantly, she adds that while she owes "my most certain art" to that hand, it is "not the art of writing, but the domestic art of knowing how to wait, to dissimulate, to pick up crumbs, rebuild . . . ," an art she compares to that of repairing porcelain. *Mes apprentissages,* p. 386.

author, and he incarnated such a figure with a calculation and savvy that prefigured Madison Avenue. It was a mystique he understood full well, since he himself possessed it when under the spell of his own would-be writing. On the other hand, Willy was able thoroughly to demystify the entire writing enterprise for Colette and his *nègres*. For if Willy did have genius, it consisted in turning writing into an assembly line activity of industrial labor; creating what Colette called his "literary industry." If, as Claude Roy pointed out, Colette accurately represents the situation of women in a capitalist society, it is equally true that Willy turned the work of all of his *nègres* into a sweatshop, in which all labor was exploited to the maximum by management. The goods which emerged from that production line were books—not Great Books, but popular books, which were read by a very large audience. Willy masterfully used sweatshop and assembly-line techniques while simultaneously playing on, and profiting from, the public's need for the Author.

Willy made his profit not only by giving the public the single, inventive author it demanded (in the figure of himself, as we have said); he also hid from that same public the mode of production from which those books emerged. For clearly, if the mystique of writing (and, therefore, the idea of the Author) is to be perpetrated, then the activity of writing must also remain mystified. Put another way, it was the insistence upon the myth of originality, upon canonized and popular literature, and upon the role of literary criticism in maintaining all of these for its own sake that Willy could to bank on, literally. He saw the hidden agenda and used it to its fullest potential.

Willy worked with his slaves by rotation. That is: he would write to one *nègre* and ask him to produce a story on a topic Willy judged fashionable. Upon receiving the text, he would send it to another *nègre* as if he had written it himself, with pleas for editing ("I have a horror of going over my own prose"). The amended text was then added onto an entirely different piece being worked on by yet another *nègre,* and so it would continue until the true authors could no longer recognize their own work. Everything appeared, of course, with the name of Willy as author. Willy was producing such a quantity of work in so many genres and areas, it was almost impossible for anyone to prove or disprove the origin of any text. Even as he posed as Author in the best romantic tradition, by his methods he altered the activity and concept of the term until it no longer had any functional meaning. As Sarde notes, Willy revived the medieval practice of collective writing. The lesson here is a paradox: the myth of originality seems to work best when its origins remain obscure.

By the time Willy had met Colette, he was already a well-known critic, journalist, satirist, and man of letters in general. The name Willy was everywhere on fin de siècle posters, pamphlets, leaflets, and tabloids. Novels, columns, essays, plays, and various other forms of writing (including a famous column of music criticism) were attributed to him, many appearing under different pen names of Willy's careful fabrication. He also had bank accounts under false names, so that he could claim poverty all of his life and frequently neglect to pay his *nègres*. Naming served Willy well.[37]

He was even, to some degree, a *nègre* himself in his "stable" of nameless writers. The poet Guillaume Apollinaire, for example, asked Willy to write his memoirs for him because, said the poet, "it would bore me." ("parce que ça m'ennuierait"). Even while the man Willy paraded around Paris, posing as author and critic extraordinaire, the name "Willy" itself became virtually a trademark, a generic label that sold books. And while most of the literati at the time were well aware that "Willy" was far from a single author producing popular novels ("Willy *have* a lot of talent," sniped Jules Renard in 1905), the public for whom Willy had nothing but disdain (if they had any taste, why would they be reading "his" lowbrow novels?) continued to buy the products and the advertising campaign.

Willy had no illusions; he knew what he was doing. "The myth of the author," he wrote, "of the solitary writer, now only exists for the public in the form of a book."[38] It is no surprise, as Joan

37. Not to mention the fact that "Will" and "Willy" are both English slang terms for penis, although, as far as I know, there is no proof that this Willy was aware of that.
38. Cited by François Caradec, *Feu Willy: avec et sans Colette* (Paris, 1984), p. 297. My translation.

Hinde Stewart notes, that the only book Willy finally revered was his account book, which he carried with him everywhere. "For M. Willy, there exists a Book, neither the book of life nor the one he never succeeds in writing, but quite simply an account-book. He keeps it scrupulously, ominously . . . Colette herself hardly ever saw 'the book' which seems to record not only Willy's eternal penury, but also her own humiliations."[39] Sarde contends that "Colette is therefore doubly alienated by her position *both* as writer-proletarian in her husband's workshops *and* as unpaid writer-wife."[40] But as Sarde notes in her 1978 biography, the sad thing is that Willy didn't even need to be present. "He exercised an inner censorship and control that extended all the way to the physical act of writing."[41]

It is from within a capitalist, production-oriented society that Colette's distaste for writing can be seen as "laziness." This she has in common with all of Willy's *nègres,* whom he was constantly threatening, cajoling, and terrorizing into producing ink-filled pages.[42] But the notion of laziness is gendered precisely when writing is viewed from its romantic, mystified perspective—the one Willy automatically assumed when he sat alone with his pen and viewed the blank page with anguish. Suddenly then, writing is no longer the crass production of popular novels, but rather an activity of the mind (not the hand) best described by, for example, Mallarmé. Then the blank page, the inability to write, the lack of "closely filled up" papers, become proofs of a neurotic genius, of a sensibility too conscious to fill pages with ink, too highstrung to engage in the work of writing, too refined to equate writing with labor.

So Colette cannot win. If she does not write, she is lazy and

39. Joan Hinde Stewart, *Colette* (Boston, 1983), p. 100.
40. Sarde, "The First Steps in a Writer's Career," p. 19. In fact, Willy did pay Colette after a while, and she even learned to demand better working conditions from her boss. The sale of the *Claudines* and their paraphernalia permitted the move to a nicer apartment. Here Colette gets her own room with a desk, lamp, and easychair, and also an exercise room for stretching her muscles. She is given a dog, a maid, a cook, and 300 francs a week.
41. Sarde, *Colette,* p. 160.
42. Several critics give complete lists of Willy's numerous *nègres,* many of whom went on to become famous in their own right. See, for example, Pierre-Robert Leclerc, "Le Moi-je de Colette," p. 786 n. 4.

unambitious, undisciplined—just like a woman. It never occurs
to anybody (except to her, in parody) to compare her distaste for
the blank page to Mallarmé's, although Willy automatically sees
his own paralysis in precisely those terms. She is a woman, after
all, who does not even desire the sacred vocation to which great
"authors" are called, and therefore presumably cannot understand its dark metaphysical turmoils. If she does write, however,
and writes in the crude working conditions provided by Willy
(four hours a day in a locked room, punching the clock, so to
speak, and having blackened pages to show for the time put in),
then she is insensitive to the high task of "Writing" and its inherent intellectual terrors.

It has been remarked that in women, ease of writing is frequently connected with easy virtue.[43] It is as if the point made by
several critics, that mass culture and its novels are seen as "feminized," were extended to the act itself of writing such novels.[44]
The more difficulty the writer has in writing, this logic would
have it, the more important the literature; and vice versa. The
first option is gendered as masculine; the second as feminine.

_____

43. Mary Trouille, "Revolution in the Boudoir: Mme Roland's Subversion of
Rousseau's Feminine Ideals," *Eighteenth-Century Life* 13 (May 1989): 78. In *La Vagabonde,* Colette's semiautobiographical character Renée Néré turns this all
around, by describing writing as a lazy luxury which she, a divorced woman
obliged to work for a living, can no longer afford. Writing, she says, means having
time to look out of the window for hours, to forget clocks and schedules, to enjoy
the laziness (*paresse*) of a corner in the couch. She concludes: "Writing takes too
much time! And furthermore, I'm not Balzac." Society now considers her, she
says, "a woman of letters who went bad" (*une femme de lettres qui a mal tourné*). *La
Vagabonde* (Paris, 1990), pp. 15–16. Colette here dramatically problematizes the
status of writing as work, and the gendered implications. Renée refers to the long
reverie which writing demands "in front of the white page" and the way treasures
are slowly unloaded onto the "virgin page." The vocabulary insists upon the Mallarmé version of writing as metaphysical crisis, as meditation; and the passage is
ironic when it juxtapositions such a notion of writing with the need to work, to
put food on the table, as well as the limitations for earning money placed upon a
single woman. Moreover, in the same passage the character adds that she can't
concentrate on writing because when someone rings to deliver coal, or the lawyer
calls, or a bill is presented, she has to answer the door and the various requests.
Daily life, in other words, intrudes—she has no servants. In this context, the daily
hours of imprisonment under the Willy regime can be seen retrospectively as
built-in protection from the intrusions of the everyday, and as guaranteed time
to daydream in order to produce the required blackened pages.
44. E.g., Huyssen, *After the Great Divide;* or Judith Williamson, "Woman is an
Island: Femininity and Colonization," in *Studies in Entertainment,* ed. Tania Modl-
eski (Bloomington, IN, 1986).

Mallarmé is, of course, a perfect model for Willy, since the poet openly celebrates (even if in anguished terms) his extreme difficulty in writing what is seen as the highest of literary projects. There can be nothing more removed from mass culture, after all, than *la poésie pure;* nothing more cerebral and Literary than seeing the choice of every word on the page as the murder of every other. But Colette is only the zealous producer of lowbrow novels which appeal to the pop culture of the day. She is a scribbler, not a writer. It is because Willy has no respect for scribblers or their prolific scribblings that he knows how to get the most out of both. Willy does not consider what any of his *nègres* (including his wife) produce to be Literature; it is merely popular fiction. The goods produced provide a pastime for the frivolous and leisured—largely women. Thus "laziness" means, finally, an inability to attain rigor of thought, and thus to produce a great work of literature.

As if to prove this point, later in her career, when Colette is established as an author of "great," not popular literature, her gender "shifts"—that is, she is described by many as a man, as if to explain her abilities. Sylvain Bonmariage, who wrote a famous anti-Colette book, says that he once told her friend Thérèse Robert that Colette smelled like a "female in rut." " 'Not at all,' Thérèse replied, 'She smells like a man . . . therein lies the magic of her seduction.' " Bonmariage himself decides that Colette was a man: "Was Colette, moreover, a woman? Certainly not, if the first attribute of a woman resides in her goodness. I always knew her to be rather mean (*méchante*), but a meanness which never had anything feminine about it."[45] And as recently as December 2, 1991, the critic Jean Chalon is reminding his readers (in *Le Figaro*) that Colette is difficult to read (and therefore a writer of importance): "It should not be forgotten that, contrary to her reputation, Colette is not an easy author. It takes several readings to fully enter her world, one that gives the appearance of the quotidian and takes you much farther, into a universe where time has suspended its flight." The subtext, of course, is that popular literature is easy to read, while great literature is not. Here again

45. Bonmariage, *Willy, Colette et moi* (Paris, 1954), pp. 19, 21.

we run into the notion of laziness and its implicit genderings. Great literature takes work to read as well as to write; popular literature is for the leisured who are by definition incapable of this type of (validated) work. Those who write it, moreover, are tacitly accused of doing so, as we have seen, with too much ease and too little effort (work). Colette, argues Chalon obliquely, belongs to great literature because she is difficult to read. The battle, in other words, is still on as to whether or not Colette is in the canon. In the *New York Times* (January 29, 1991), to cite another example, Michiko Kakutani begins a review of a new Colette biography with the following sentence: "Although Colette is mainly known to Americans as the author of such gently risqué entertainments as 'Gigi' and 'Chéri,' she had achieved widespread popular and critical recognition in France by her death in 1954." Colette herself complained to her friends Jean Denoël and Marthe Lamy about the popularity of her two "easiest" works: "After all, I am not just the author of *Claudine* and *Chéri*" ("Je n'ai quand même pas écrit que *Claudine* et *Chéri!*"). Her complaint is meant to insist upon her less popular and more difficult texts as proof of her importance as a writer.

Claudine à l'école was not an instant success, but Willy was a master at advertising, an early genius of publicity, as we noted earlier, and especially of self-promotion. He planted good reviews in major Parisian newspapers—some written by him under other pseudonyms, some by friends such as the influential journalist and courtisane Rachilde (in *Le Mercure*), Gaston Deschamps (in *Le Temps*), and Pierre Brisson (in *Les Annales*). After that, the book sold forty thousand copies in two months.

Willy had been determined to achieve a financial coup with this book: not only had he come up with the idea, he had also arranged for the book to have a tantalizing cover: a young, sensuous girl in wooden shoes sitting on a desk (Willy used the Little Red Riding Hood illustration from Emilio della Sudda). Initially finding the text of what was to become *Claudine à l'école* insufficiently salacious, Willy had suggested (and perhaps even himself added) a few lesbian and other libidinous overtones, particularly with regard to the headmistress. "Don't be afraid of being spicy," he had told Colette—but apparently the young, still very provincial Colette had not been quite spicy enough, and had been duly "edited." The extent of Willy's emendations remains unclear, since the manuscript was destroyed (like Descartes's "Olympica"). Such a loss further fuels the originality/ownership controversy, of course.[46] Willy was to claim (echoed by his friend Bonmariage) that the changes he made were numerous and justified a co-authorship role. Colette, of course, would protest throughout her life that all Willy did to the *Claudines* was add a few vulgar words to her text, and quite a few corrections in the margin. Yet she always maintained that he was an excellent critic and judge of talent, and that he would have made a superb editor-in-chief.

The fin de siècle was fond of autobiography, erotic (preferably bisexual) protagonists, sensuality in general, and a sort of verbal impressionism (which is how, much later, Cocteau and others were to characterize Colette's style). Proust, of course, is the most obvious example of the period.[47] Willy made sure that all of these components were well in evidence in the first *Claudine*. He also made clever use of illustrations.

In the 1820s in France the *beau livre* had been a luxury item, something roughly the equivalent of what is today called the "art book." The popularity of these expensive editions was probably inspired by that of romanticism, and continued throughout the nineteenth century. But such books were mainly available to the rich and to collectors because of their prohibitive price. What was

46. Colette, in her introduction to the *Claudine* series for the Flammarion *Oeuvres complètes* (Paris, 1948–50), says that Willy had asked Paul Barlet (friend, secretary, and *nègre*) to destroy all of the *Claudine* manuscripts. He destroyed the first two, but gave the third and fourth (*Claudine en ménage* and *Claudine s'en va*) to Colette. See the 1984 Pléiade *Oeuvres*, p. 1241. The mystery persists, however; sightings have been reported, including one in the Pléiade edition, which places a footnote to the anecdote as told by Colette: "Nevertheless, one occasionally hears of the first two *Claudine* manuscripts. Several years ago, they were said to be in Belgium" (ibid.). This note not only continues the mystique and obsession regarding the Colette-Willy literary venture but throws doubt on Colette's version."

47. The fin de siècle is usually described as spanning the 1880s to 1903 or 1904, and as a time of degeneration caused by economic uncertainty. The belle époque covers the years of economic growth just before the First World war, from 1904–1914. Colette's career includes and goes well beyond both of these. See Eugene Weber, *France, Fin de Siècle* (Cambridge, MA, 1986), pp. 10–11, which refer to the fin de siècle as a time of "national and cultural degeneration." See also Theodore Zeldin, *France 1848–1945*, vol. 5, *Anxiety and Hypocrisy* (New York, 1981); and Elaine Showalter, *Sexual Anarchy: Gender and Culture at the Fin de Siècle* (New York, 1990).

innovative about them, among other things, was the fact that they foregrounded illustrations, which became at least as important, and took up as much space, as the accompanying text. When lithography came to replace more elaborate forms of illustration, however, the *beau livre* became a vanishing genre. The *livre de peintre* appeared at the end of the nineteenth century as a more affordable alternative. Being cheaper, lithographs further revolutionized the notion of illustrations and their relation to the text. Popular literature at the turn of the century in France drew its inspiration from these earlier, highly illustrated and highly cultured ancestors. Popular literature was intensely and obsessively illustrated. One of its forms was the "demi-luxe" edition, a book equivalent of the contemporary *demi mondaine:* not respectable enough to be considered high class, but too beautiful to be considered trash.[48]

The fin de siècle's obsession with illustrations included advertisements—the *réclames* which were splashed all over Paris in the form of huge posters, painted walls, signs, tabloids, pamphlets, leaflets, painted ashtrays, water pitchers, and so on. (The word *réclame* took on its present meaning, as advertisement, in the mid-nineteenth century.) Willy smelled this fascination with images and exploited it (which helped to earn him the nickname of "Monsieur Réclamier"). He helped launch a series of trinkets connected with the character Claudine. Some of them concretized, as it were, the illustrations from the book: the Claudine hat, the famous Claudine collar, the Claudine haircut. These became all the rage (an equivalent in more recent time, for example, of the gadgets, trinkets, and clothing—to name a few—spawned by any "blockbuster" movie). Willy not only created *réclames* for *Claudine à l'école,* he not only transported the book's illustrations from the text to the street; he expanded on them as well. Thus he produced the usual posters and leaflets, but also more fanciful talismans such as Claudine perfume, Claudine lotion, and even Claudine cigarettes. He encouraged the public's fetishization of

48. On Colette's relationship to her illustrators, and to illustrations, see Anne-Marie Christin's "Colette et ses illustrateurs," in *Colloque de Cérisy,* 1988, *Cahiers Colette,* no. 11 (Société des amis de Colette, 1989), pp. 171–90.

Claudine herself by producing a metonymic economy of Claudine paraphernalia.

It was in the postcard series that he launched in connection with the book that Willy surpassed himself. These postcards exploit the fin de siècle fascination with pictures and images in general, but they simultaneously play on the period's interest in biography, and in prurient, if oblique, eroticism.[49] The postcards are all photographs, most of which show Colette ("Madame Willy") dressed as Claudine. The truth then is revealed in the guise of a masquerade, since Colette *was* Claudine to a large degree.[50] At the same time, however, Colette is depicted as the invention of Willy, who is himself posing in many of these postcards. Willy could never resist propagating and enjoying his own image. As Colette put it, part of his megalomania was "the obsession with describing himself, the love of contemplating himself. It never left him and assumed a variety of forms, in which the public saw only an unbridled flair for publicity."[51] Colette's theory seems fairly self-evident: Willy, being unable to write (Colette's word is *stérile*), transgressed the normal bounds of what she calls "commercial opportunity." It was as if, with this obsessive propagation of his image everywhere in Paris, begun as a genuine attempt to sell "his" books, he were compensating for the damaged vanity of the failed great Author.

If Colette's father tried to "cover up" the blank page by binding volumes and giving them titles, Willy's method is to blacken the streets and shops of Paris with his picture or with pictures of what he has convinced everyone are his literary creations. The postcards, although very successful (the book sells more and more copies), begin to show the desperate measures Willy takes to hide his "sterility," his inability to bear texts. It should come as no sur-

49. For an excellent article on postcards of Paris in the period, see Naomi Schor, "*Cartes Postales:* Representing Paris in 1900," *Critical Inquiry* 18 (Winter 1992): 188–244.

50. See, e.g., Danielle Deltel, "Journal manqué, autobiographie masquée: *Claudine à l'école* de Colette," *Revue des sciences humaines* 73 no. 192 (October–December, 1983): 47–71. Deltel argues that Colette's first novel occupies a position somewhere between the journal and the monologue (p. 71). See also Michel Mercier, "Colette et le pur objet de l'écriture" in the *Colloque de Cérisy,* pp. 94 ff.

51. Colette, *Mes apprentissages,* p. 377.

prise, therefore, that the major iconic metaphor of the postcards is fathering.

In a dizzying but brilliantly organized representation, one card shows Colette as Claudine, dressed in the famous Claudine school uniform. In the background stands Willy, in full formal dress complete with top hat. Colette is seen sketching Willy, as if she were paying homage to her "creator" by drawing him in his own image of himself. For Willy himself as a fictional character is his only real creation: he manages to invent himself in the image of author desired by his reading public and cultivated by the literary establishment itself. The fact that Colette is the author of *Claudine à l'école*, that her book bears her husband's name and not hers, and that *he* is *her* inspiration for the book and not she his, is successfully belied by the postcard with its blatant semiology of patriarchy. Willy is depicted as the master of the text, of the wife, and of the protagonist. He is the supreme originator; father both of Claudine and, by extension, of Colette, since she is posing as Claudine.

The postcard, like all others in the series, is a blatant and conscious parody of gender stereotyping in 1900, and in the literary world in particular. It pokes fun at such stereotypes in a farcical, obvious fashion (in other postcards, Colette is seen kneeling at her husband's feet, or praying to him). It also makes a mockery of the notion of author—not only for the obvious tacit reasons (e.g., this author doesn't write); but also for overt reasons: in his regalia dress and dignified pose he is a perfect cartoon of "the Author," a Nadar (who did in fact photograph him) photographic portrait of fakery. Much is said of early belle époque culture—its view of women, for example, or of writing—when we consider that in spite of the near slapstick aspect to these cards, they were never seen as particularly humorous and were sold in unbelievable numbers.

The titles of these postcards are equally provocative. Some are labeled "Colette et Willy," giving the viewer a partial, voyeuristic glimpse of their "real life" marriage. Another is called "Claudine," and another, "Willy and Claudine." The person whose name is always confused, in other words, is Colette's (who, it should be remembered, is still not being called by her first name nor by a name she has chosen for herself even when she is referred to as "Colette"). In another card, which seems chronologically to follow the one in which Colette is sketching Willy, she appears as having just finished drawing him. Under her drawing, in huge letters, she has scrawled, "Ça c'est Willy," and the beginnings of "her" signature, "Claud . . ." Her signature is that of the character she has created; the iconography of the card, however, turns it all around: she is undersigning, as it were, the official version that Willy established of, first, his own identity ("this is Willy") and, second, hers, which is as splintered as "her" name on the drawing. All the postcards show Colette-Claudine as a naughty, sensuous schoolgirl, attempting (and not always succeeding) to "copy" the character in the book. When Willy is present in the postcard, Colette is depicted as utterly submissive, entirely in his shadow.

As should be clear at this point, there are inherently contradictory assumptions concerning "originality": its insistence upon spontaneous (ex nihilo, because unprecedented) creation on the one hand, and its simultaneous metaphors of texts as offspring, authors as fathers, and literary canon as ancestry on the other. This contradiction at the heart of originality—the necessity and concomitant negation of genealogy—was one that Willy seems to have grasped intuitively. Seen in this light, his postcards are publicity ploys that unwittingly trace the paradox of originality in its fin de siècle context. In one postcard, for example, he is shown standing alone, with the caption: "Willy, father of the Claudines."

The ambiguity of identity and authorship were combined in the *réclames*, as *Claudine à l'école*, buoyed by its popular success, became a series.[52] In 1901, Willy discovered a dancehall performer who was using the name of Emilie Zouzé. True to form, Willy gave her another name, "Polaire," and arranged for her to play Claudine in the theater version of the second novel in the series, *Claudine à Paris*. He became her lover, insinuated that Colette was her lover as well, and paraded about town with both women dressed as Claudine. (In another reversal—life imitating art imi-

---

52. *Claudine à l'école* is followed one year later by *Claudine à Paris* (1901), *Claudine en ménage* (1902), *Claudine s'en va* (1903), all signed by Willy.

tating text, and so on—Colette cut her hair at Willy's request so that she could look more like her own heroine. Sido was thoroughly displeased, feeling that twenty years of labor had landed on the floor.) Thus Willy, playing a sort of Daddy Warbucks combined with gigolo, ménage à trois sponsor, and above all, Author, literally staged a moving illustration from the series called Claudine. In this iconology, Colette as Claudine mimes the "real" Claudine, Polaire, who was playing Claudine on the stage with great popular acclaim. A cartoon which ran in the major papers showed Willy playing Pygmalion with little Claudine dolls resembling Colette and "Polaire." Colette is then three times removed from the character she is supposed to copy. The representation at work here, in other words, insists upon maintaining the distance between Colette and her own text: she is never in a direct relationship or lineage; conversely, she is always derivative of the original and, ironically enough, even of the copy Polaire. Colette is copy of the copy, and never in an economy of genealogy or of origin implicit in the notion of authorship.

The trinkets (including inkwells in the form of Willy's top hat), postcards, posters, statuettes of Claudine, beauty products, and so on—are external equivalents of the psychological fetishization (or *tripotage,* "pawing": Willy is fondling the Claudine dolls in the Pygmalion cartoon) that Willy visits upon Colette's body and prose. The appropriation is at every level: textual, personal, political, social, and sexual. But Colette is, after all, only one of many *nègres* who served Willy's narcissism; his goal had nothing to do with her. It had more to do with the displacement offered him by the *réclames* he propagated in lieu of texts. These advertisements were supplemented by caricatures: such famous cartoonists as Bac and Rib drew him frequently, and thus added to the Willy image. Willy also demanded that he appear in recognizable fashion in the later *Claudines.* The character Henri Maugis, the music critic and wit, is the charitable portrait of her husband which Colette duly produced. All this réclamage affords Willy an acceptable form of self-fetishization, which would be impossible without the public's parallel fetishization of the Author. It is in this sense, and for this reason, that what Willy does and how he does it are important here.

When the journalist Rachilde guessed her role in the *Claudines,* Colette wrote to her in a panic, "Heavens no, do not name me in Claudine! For family reasons, convention, relationships, bla bla bla . . . For Willy alone. For Willy all of the glory." We have noted here more than once that, from the beginning, the name is at issue in the Colette story. First, at the simplest level: Willy renames those around him, including his wife, Polaire, and himself. The name also becomes an issue for the rights and recognition of Colette as author. Colette finally stops using the name "Willy" as a signature to her work in 1904 with the publication of *Dialogues de bêtes.* But she signs it "Colette Willy," thus doubly inscribed by patriarchy. Meanwhile critics emit, without irony, such statements as "This is the first book to bear Colette's own name, Colette Willy." Or "Colette took off the mask and wrote in her own name."[53]

Colette signs "Willy" until 1904, "Colette Willy" until 1913, and "Colette (Colette Willy)" until 1923, when at last she is published as "Colette." In 1907, one year after Colette and Willy had separated, he sold the rights to the Claudines for very little money.[54] "Is it true, is it possible," she writes to her soon to be former husband, "that all of the *Claudines* and the two *Minne* are now the property of editors? Is it possible that all of that is lost forever for you and for me? In the name of heaven, tell me the truth for once. Is it possible that those books which are so dear to me are lost forever?"[55] So long as the books were in Colette's control, even if signed by her husband, she felt them to be her own. But when Willy sold the rights, Colette "lost" the books "forever," and never forgave Willy for that loss. That he publicly claimed her work was something to which she had agreed. That he sold her work, without her permission and without consulting her, she could not forgive. She never spoke to him again; but she certainly wrote letters. The insult here, of course, is that her product is validated, of course because it is profitable; but she is left with neither recognition nor recourse. In the eyes of the law,

53. Marks, *Colette,* p. 175.

54. For the details of this sale, including publishers and prices, see Colette, *Oeuvres* (Pléiade ed.), 1:xcvi.

55. Ibid., p. xcvii.

she is neither owner nor even coauthor of her own work; in the eyes of the public, she is a virtual unknown as an author. She is left witnessing various "Claudine" spinoffs, which she is power-less to restrain. And the newspapers of the day take sides: *Paris-Journal* is for Willy; *Paris Théâtre* for Colette.

"One would think," Colette raged to Léon Hamel, "that he wanted not only to get very little money out of them, but also to make sure that *never,* even after his death, would I regain posses-sion of those books which are mine."[56] It was, in fact, after her own death that Colette was to lose, once again, her position as sole author of the *Claudines.*

In 1907, before Colette learned that her husband had sold the rights to her books, she and Willy had prepared—and she had written—an announcement to the reader. Signed by Willy and written as if by him, the announcement states that the Willy-Colette "collaboration" has come to an end, and that the books which had appeared under his name would henceforth be signed "Willy and Colette Willy." This agreement appeared as a preface to all Claudine books as of 1907.[57] Beginning in 1948, however, Colette won her battle on rights, and after that year her earlier books appeared only with the name "Colette." Justice seemed to have been done, as Colette's friend the great violinist Hélène Jourdan-Morhange is said to have exclaimed upon learning this new state of affairs.[58]

But in 1955, one year after Colette's death, Willy's son Jacques insisted that the "bilateral agreement" of 1907 be honored, and that his father's pseudonym be returned to the title pages of all Claudines. As of 1955, then, all of Colette's early work appears under the names "Colette and Willy." Publication rights, owner-ship rights, and marital rights are at stake in this controversy. So deep a vein does it touch in the literary establishment that every edition of Colette's early works, every biography, every collection

56. Cited by Sarde, "The First Steps in a Writer's Career," pp. 18–19.

57. See *Oeuvres* (Pléiade ed.), 1:xcviii, for the full text of this agreement.

58. Cited in Maurice Bouvier-Ajam, "Willy et Colette Willy," *Europe: revue lit-téraire mensuelle,* nos. 631–32 (special issue on Colette, November–December 1981): 52–54.

of her works (including the most recent, and highly dignified new Pléiade edition) feels compelled to discuss the controversy, take sides, decide whether it is Colette or Willy who is more believable in this instance as over that, and so on. Not only, as we noted at the outset of this chapter, do critics fall into the "feminist" camp or the "Willy" camp. Colette's public letters and autobiographical comments on this matter, and Willy's printed and reported self-defenses, are as if continued in the criticism. The controversy cannot be laid to rest, it seems. Colette's originality is continually put into question in the terms propagated by the mythology of originality: purity, authenticity, totality, subject sovereignty. Her stature in the canon is therefore perpetually at stake. What professes to be a debate about whether Willy remembers better than Colette does (on how much he changed her text, for example), whether he authored the Claudines as much as he said or as little as Colette claimed, is in fact a struggle about the continued importance of originality itself in any assessment of a literary text. When the canonical Pléiade edition questions Colette's version as over Willy's, chooses one over the other, accuses both of omissions or poor memory, what is ultimately being protected is the very image of the Author (original, but also singular, unique, and autonomous) that Willy so masterfully mimed and profited from.

When *Claudine à l'école* first appeared, in 1900, it was the year of the Paris "Universal Exposition" and, for most students of the period, close to the beginning of the belle époque as well. Willy was at the height of his popularity, so much a product of the period that he seemed to thrive in tandem with the belle époque itself. (In 1927, when the belle époque had come to a complete end, Willy's stature had been completely destroyed as well.)[59] "His" novel, *Claudine à l'école*, was considered to be the *Liaisons*

59. A single anecdote demonstrates Willy's importance when his popularity was at its height. Beginning in 1889, Willy was a music critic, writing (in part, at least) a column called "Lettres de l'ouvreuse," which he signed "Une Ouvreuse du cirque d'été" and which dominated the music scene in Paris for about twenty years. In 1904, Willy had an altercation at a Lamoureux concert with the composer Erik Satie, whom Willy had attacked mercilessly in his "L'Ouvreuse" column. When Satie punched him, Willy responded by beating the composer with a cane. Satie was unceremoniously thrown out of the concert hall, solely (and without question) on Willy's demand. Cited by Caradec, *Feu Willy*, pp. 47–49.

dangereuses of its day. Certainly, the bawdy eroticism and farcical elements in the novel, coupled with its journal/epistolary style, are reminiscent of the Choderlos de Laclos novel.

In Willy's preface to *Claudine à l'école,* however, the novel he attempts to echo is not *Les liaisons dangereuses,* but Rousseau's *Julie, ou la nouvelle Héloïse.* Rousseau's own preface to that novel is an extremely complicated bit of prose. On the one hand, Rousseau uses the convention of the epistolary novel preface: he claims that these letters have fallen into his hands by chance, that he is only the editor and has made minor changes (in landscape, proper names, style), and that he had initial doubts about publishing this work, which "with its 'gothic' tone is more appropriate for women than are philosophy books."[60] All these elements are to be found in most prefaces to epistolary novels (including that of Choderlos de Laclos), where the author poses as editor and claims, for purposes of verisimilitude which are quickly parodied (*Les liaisons dangereuses* is one such parody), to be responsible only for minor changes and for deciding to publish the work in question.

But Rousseau's preface also purposely risks tearing at the fabric of the verisimilitude it insists upon.[61] The "editor" warns us that although he bears merely the title of editor, he has worked on this book himself and will not hide this fact (*je ne m'en cache pas*). He then commits another *mise en abîme* of sorts, by suggesting as unlikely what is in fact true: that the correspondence that forms the novel is nothing more than his invention (*une fiction*). Then, addressing his readers in the context of their corruption (as he puts it), he turns it around again and snaps, "the book is certainly a fiction for you." The reader of Rousseau's book is, in other words, already so corrupted by the times that he will take as fiction the moralistic idealism of the young couple whose story the "letters" tell. Thus Rousseau plays with fiction/truth by turning each into the other, and plays with his position of author by insisting that he is no more than the editor and simultaneously

60. *Julie, ou la nouvelle Héloïse* (Paris, 1960), p. 4. "Ce receuil avec son gothique ton convient mieux aux femmes que les livres de philosophie" (my translation).

61. The Afterword, dubbed a Preface, which closes *Julie,* similarly puts the boundaries of fiction and authorship into question.

hinting that he may have written it all (*Ai-je fait le tout, et la correspondence entière est-elle une fiction?*).

Rousseau's preface, then, brilliantly undermines all of the assumptions concerning fiction and the role of the author. As Baudelaire will do a century later, Rousseau insults and threatens his readers as he tells them what they will and will not think as they read him. More importantly, he claims that this work is for women, and that it may even be useful to those with "unstable lives" (*une vie déreglée*) who still care for honesty. On the other hand, chaste young women do not read novels, an intrinsically corrupt genre, and especially not this one (*Jamais fille chaste n'a lu de romans*). In the midst of this rather dizzying tirade, Rousseau says, "every honest man must admit to the books he publishes. I therefore place my name at the beginning of this collection, not to appropriate it, but to answer for it" *(Tout honnête homme doit avouer les livres qu'il publie. Je me nomme donc à la tête de ce receuil, non pour me l'approprier, mais pour en répondre).* The declaration that one should admit to one's books—coupled with the refusal to assume the position of owner (appropriator), and therefore of author—succeeds in creating a paradox which makes responsibility impossible to assign, even as the sentence professes concern for nothing but. Responsibility belongs to the editor, but in name only; it is the author's, but we are unsure if he is the same as the editor; and it is the reader's because she or he is part of the corruption of the times that makes for such unfortunate books in the first place. Thus, as with Baudelaire, the reader is condemned along with the book before he has even begun to read it. So too, the preface is only posing as extratextual, or paratext; ultimately it is an integral part of the narrative.

I have lingered over Rousseau's preface to his *Julie* for two main reasons: first, because it demonstrates a convention of the eighteenth-century epistolary novel, a convention that Willy will use to the fullest; and, second, because this preface, though preaching responsibility, refuses to assume any responsibility of authorship. Rousseau denies having authored his own text; but at the same time he insists he has done so. Once again, Willy will use this same ploy—except that in Willy's case the question of responsibility and authorship has different stakes.

Willy, too, claims that a manuscript fell into his hands. He was nervous about reading it because it was wrapped in pink, a sign of feminine manuscripts (*les manuscrits féminins*).[62] But his fears are quickly allayed when he discovers that it is a young girl's journal (the logic here is less than limpid; one supposes that the education—in more than one sense—of a young woman is far more interesting to Willy and his public than merely "feminine prose," which Willy calls *papotages syrupeux*). Echoing Rousseau directly, Willy says that the book is by a young girl, but not for young girls (*De jeune fille, mais non pour jeune filles*). With Rousseau, he links the novel to the decadence of his period, and cites a canon of lascivious novels of the day. The difference, of course, is that Willy uses this catalogue with a disgust which is clearly feigned; in fact, he is whetting his reader's appetite by placing *Claudine à l'école* in such risqué company.[63] (Rousseau, on the other hand, despite his protestations concerning the baseness of the novel, suggests that *Julie* overcomes the genre's inherent corruption because of the moral integrity of its characters.)

Like Rousseau, Willy claims that the correspondence he is publishing contains rustic phrases and mannerisms that may shock the city dweller. Rousseau warns his reader to be patient with the grammatical errors, flat tone, and clichés. His letter writers are provincial, he says; children with "romanesque" imaginations. So Willy accuses Claudine of a flatness (*Elle note tout sur le même plan*). She is a child (*une âme non formée*), who writes with a provincial brutality (*une franchise compagnarde un peu brutale*). Like Rousseau, Willy has had to work on the manuscript, and has cut a few of such brutalities. And Willy's preface even contains a literary apostrophe to Rousseau: "this little Claudine who is almost a child of Nature—oh Rousseau—seems to me, in fact, almost innocent in her ingenuous perversion."

Rousseau uses "gothic" and "romanesque" in the sense of the

---

62. *Oeuvres* (Pléiade ed.), 1: 3–5. All references to the preface are to these pages. It should be added that Rousseau himself actually wrote his novel on beautiful paper, tied in "feminine" ribbons. Here too Willy apes his predecessor.

63. He also suggests that the novel belongs to the pornographic industry which flourished in Belgium as a result of the severe censorship imposed by the Second Empire in France. Some books, indeed, were published in France but professed publication in Belgium to avoid legal difficulties.

late eighteenth century: at odds with the norm—in this case, socially deviant. Willy uses the equivalent for 1899: *sauvageonne* (savagelike), thus eliciting Rousseauist tendencies: deviating from a norm that is ultimately itself questioned and held responsible for the moral difficulties in which a young, innocent girl finds herself. Claudine is not, Willy argues, immoral, but amoral. Like Julie, Claudine has no mother, which is meant to explain why she lacks guidance and support.[64]

As is well known, the novel of letters flourished in eighteenth-century England and France, to name only two national literatures, precisely because the novel was considered a base genre. A collection of letters, on the other hand, could pose as historical, as real. It behooved the actual author of such "letters," therefore, to uphold the verisimilitude of the collection by inventing a story of discovery, generally recounted in the preface. How the letters fell into his hands established both their veracity *as* letters and his role as merely editor and (at times) publisher. The author denied that he was anything but the facilitator of the collection; above all, he was not the author. The epistolary convention, in other words, consists in the author denying authorship. By the time Rousseau publishes *Julie,* such a convention can already be manipulated: Rousseau, as we have seen, flirts with authorship but finally stays behind a less than convincing mask as editor.

What Willy has done is a prose tour de force: he has used the canonical language, convention, and protestations of the epistolary genre to install himself as author. Skillfully maneuvering within a rhetoric of double irony, as William Empson used to term such ploys, he has baldly stated the truth within a context that virtually assures the reader's disbelief. As with the readers of *Julie,* the more Willy insists that he is not the author of *Claudine à l'école,* the more his readers will believe that he is. It is the ruse of Molière's Tartuffe, the greatest of literary hypocrites, who frequently and calmly utters the phrase "I am not an angel," eliciting nothing but admiration from his gullible patron.

64. Claudine is explicit concerning the school in which she has been put by her father: "si j'avais une maman, je sais bien qu'elle ne me laisserait pas vingt-quatre heures ici" (p. 10).

Nevertheless, there is something vaguely disquieting about such self-exposure. The editors at Ollendorf are nervous. On February 1, 1900, the publisher Pierre Valdagne writes to Willy:

> My dear friend, I have read your preface and asked Ollendorf to read it as well. We both feel that it has the considerable flaw of letting the reader think this novel is not your own. Do you really think the preface is useful? It slows the reader down, emphasizes the salacious . . . in short, if you have a moment we would very much like to talk to you about it.[65]

Willy's notes to himself on Valdagne's letter demonstrate that he knew exactly what he was doing. He scribbled: "Answered. A) Preface useful because it exculpates Claudine. B) Frequently used literary artifice. Examples of." Willy's arguments apparently convinced the publisher, since the novel appeared with the preface intact. He demonstrated to his publisher that the literary convention of denying authorship only serves to reinforce the reader's conviction that he is being duped, and that the "editor" is of course the author. No doubt one of the "examples of" must have been Rousseau. By making conscious allusion to the Rousseau preface of the eighteenth-century best seller *Julie,* Willy further manipulates the French reader. Claudine will become, just as Willy had hoped, the Julie of her own time: the virgin on the edge of sexual knowledge and adult love, whose descriptions of her society lead the reader inexorably to blame the mores of the day, and not the heroine.

Willy seems to have made himself believe that he had actually "created" Claudine. He had thought up the idea; had lent his trademark name to *Claudine à l'école,* thus ensuring that it would at least be noticed; had framed the book in a brilliantly crafted preface; had invented, controlled, and disseminated advertisements for the novel; had launched trinkets and postcards to further catapult its success; and finally had made himself a living example of the Author about town. The concept was his, as he always maintained; Colette merely executed it; she did the labor for Willy's design.

It is perhaps because the notion of author rests upon that of

---

65. *Oeuvres* (Pléiade ed.), 1:1254 (my translation).

"first cause," or idea, that Willy laid claims to Claudine. It is also, of course, because he was unable to write that he appropriated Claudine and the ensuing success. Nevertheless, the legal arguments, counterarguments, and bitterness surrounding their marriage and the reason for its end all center on Claudine, on who had rights to her, who created her. When Willy sold the publishing rights, he was not only affirming himself as author; he was also making it impossible for Colette to rectify the situation. As we have seen, she finally lost the legal battle she thought she had won: she did not own the rights to her early books, and so risked losing the right to put her name on the title page as author. Her legal difficulties in this regard mirror the assumptions concerning authorship: it is a first-cause economy, as we have noted, one in which a "woman" by definition within this context cannot fit. Because Colette is a woman, her authorship is always at issue, always contested.

"Every honest man must admit to the books he publishes," Rousseau had written in his own preface. It is not by chance that Rousseau is here obliquely alluding to an honest man's recognition of illegitimate children—a recognition to which Rousseau, in his own life, rarely acceded. The connection constantly made between genealogy and literary tradition, between ancestry and literary predecessors, between progenitor and literary offspring is not without significance. Willy imposes the implications of Rousseau's dictum onto Colette's writing: as with an illegitimate child, the mother undertakes the gestation and production. But it is the father who is able to give the child its name, social standing, and legitimacy. *Claudine à l'école,* according to this logic, is nothing without Willy's name on it, the man who referred to himself as "the father of Claudine." Indeed, the ubiquitous genealogical and therefore male metaphors that characterize the notion of author make it nearly impossible for women to inscribe themselves within its bounds.

Not coincidentally, it is Rousseau who gives us one of the best mythologies of the author's inception. The *Confessions* tell of the famous moment under the tree when the thirty-seven-year-old Rousseau, who had barely written a line in his life, was suddenly inspired to become the great Rousseau we know today. The vagueness of the "event," and its spectacular consequences (many of which were already known by the time Rousseau was writing this part of the *Confessions*) serve to enhance, rather than to elucidate, the mythology of the author. Rousseau describes his experience as a conversion to the vocation of writer; as an epiphany which, precisely because it produces a first, an original concept, and even a birth, is also necessarily *ex nihilo,* and therefore impossible, like all moments of grace, to explicate.

Walking along the road to Vincennes (Rousseau is in "no condition to pay for cabs"), it will be recalled, he has with him the *Mercure de France;* glancing through it (the chance aspect is like that of Proust), he sees the Dijon Academy's question for the prize: "Has the progress of the sciences and arts done more to corrupt morals or to improve them?"[66]

The revelation is instantaneous: "The moment I read this I beheld another universe and became another man." But we are disappointed if we want to know how this revelation functions: "The details have escaped me," Rousseau tells us. He has already written about this event, and one of the "peculiarities" of his memory is that as soon as he "commits its burden to paper," it "deserts" him. He does remember that by the time he reached Vincennes, he was "in a state of agitation bordering on delirium" (mirroring Descartes's state after the day of meditation that led to the dreams). Diderot encourages him to write, and Rousseau adds (in the histrionic tone permeating the *Confessions*), "And from that moment I was lost. All the rest of my life and of my misfortunes followed inevitably as a result of that moment's madness."

Like many revelations, that moment, which turns Rousseau into a writer, occurs in a flash but then breaks down into various miniflashes. Initially there is the experience of reading the Dijon question; then the first part of the writing is done "in pencil under an oak tree"; that in turn causes a "fermentation" and intensity to go into motion, which were to last for "more than four or five years." Moreover, the composition of the famous "first" essay spawns a method of writing that Rousseau tells us he has "almost

---

66. This and all other quotations concerning this incident are taken from *The Confessions,* trans. J. M. Cohen (Harmondsworth, U.K., 1985), pp. 327–329.

always followed" since. The method is dictation, which Rousseau resorts to because he meditates at night on his writing and has quickly found that "the break caused by my getting up and dressing [makes] me lose everything." He hires a secretary. "When she arrived I dictated to her from my bed my work of the preceding night." This method, he says, has saved "much that I might otherwise have forgotten." What is clear here is that writing reflects the contents of a sacred, spontaneous moment which, if interrupted by daily life, is lost forever. And although Rousseau tells us that his nightly meditations entail "incredible labor," they occur with eyes closed and need to be instantly recorded, much as dreams (Descartes, Freud) are lost upon waking. Writing is the tool which fashions the idea, and can in fact be undertaken by anybody (a secretary, for example).

Rousseau is willing to allow the concept of labor into his work as writer. There is the "incredible labor" already mentioned, which occurs in the night with the reshaping of sentences and the meditations; and then there is the work of correcting the text once the moment of inspiration is past and has been recorded. Obviously, these are very different types of labor. The first is a childbirth that produces a fragile idea, which consciousness must rush to make permanent. The second is menial and, like writing itself, can be done by anybody who has studied grammar, syntax, and so on. This first essay of his, Rousseau comments, "though full of strength and fervour," was lacking "in logic and order," and so Diderot "suggested a few corrections." Rousseau concludes this originary narrative with a telling phrase: "Whatever talents one may have been born with, the art of writing is not learned all at once."

Talent and the art of writing, then, are very different activities. "Talent" is like grace, befalling the true "author" without his understanding it or controlling it. One has it or one doesn't. "The art of writing," on the other hand, is a learned activity, one which entails "logic and order." Talent is in terror of being interrupted by the likes of daily life; writing itself partakes of the quotidian. It is original thought—that most obscure and mysterious of all experiences, and yet the sine qua non of any genuine "author"— which remains outside the confines of the "real world." The fact that such a view is logocentric is the least of our problems here: what we are pointing to is a division of labor on substantive and hierarchical grounds. One kind of labor ("talent") sees itself as resonant with the conversion experiences of a Paul or an Augustine, as happening "all at once"; the other ("the act of writing") belongs to a Madame Levasseur, the secretary who takes dictation, and cannot be learned "all at once." The first is a sacred vocation; the second a learned skill.[67] It is the epiphany that matters and that the writing tries to recapture.

Given the masculinist metaphysics of the originary, to which I have been pointing throughout this chapter, we can repeat the prior claims thus: in the myth of the original genius, as it is imagined in Western terms, the idea and the labor involved in its formulation as idea are gendered as the purview of men with talent. Menial labor belongs to ordinary men and to women. In this sense, then, the two writings are in place, as we have been using them here—Writing as the moment of revelation (Pascal's "In Memoriam," for example), coming as close as possible to the instant of grace (the comments penciled under the oak tree); and writing as scribing, as industry.

Colette remains secular: she refuses to see writing as a vocation or calling; she does not privilege or mystify the Idea or inspiration; she insists that writing entails a single form of labor, no different from making shoes. "I thought that the task of writing," she notes in *Le Fanal bleu*, "was like any other chore. You put down your tool and joyfully cry 'finished.'" Talent is not the property of the unique individual; it can be learned, and Colette sees herself as having attained it through work. Such an attitude facilitates the destabilization of her status as "Author," and the concomitant reluctance with which she is admitted to the literary canon.[68] She is, after all, exploding nothing less than the ori-

67. I emphasize this distinction because, in the mythology of the Author, daily life is frequently inscribed as the devil in the otherwise Edenic realm of original thought. For example, Coleridge claimed that the knocking on the door (of a salesman?) prevented him from finishing "Kubla Khan," a poem that was complete in his thoughts.

68. I will note here, since autobiographical remarks seem both tolerated and almost de rigueur at present, that when I took my Ph.D. exams at Berkeley in 1974, I was told to remove Colette from my list of Great Books. She was not, I was told, a great author; she was a producer of popular (read: unimportant) litera-

ginary narratives on origin. If woman is inscribed as derivative, as always Adam's rib, in the Western metaphysical text—that is, as eternally unable to partake of what is understood as "original"—Colette's pooh-poohing of Writing as over writing, of the very notion of the original genius, of a privileged labor, insists upon a concept of writing as work, and work based as much on hours put in as on "talent." Far from needing to dictate her fragile night thoughts upon awakening, Colette wrote for a given number of hours a day, much as one would punch the clock in a factory. To Rousseau's rhapsodic metaphors about original thought (fermentation, frenzy, passion, agitation bordering on delirium, enthusiasm—all words used to describe what for Rousseau is the indescribable moment), Colette proposes metaphors of factory life, craft (the tool), homework. She refuses to deny the drudgery of writing; she refuses to exclude writing from everydayness; she integrates the workplace into her home; she professes bland incredulity at notions of hierarchized labor and privileged writing. What she finally does, then, is to resist any distinction between high and mass culture in literary terms, or between a Mallarmé and a Maupassant. She measures writing in quantity, just as Willy had measured her own output. She calls, in other words, Willy's bluff.

Colette's open refusal to adhere to the mystique of the Author had its consequences: she was, and remains, marginalized in the literary hegemony.[69] Such a position of ambiguity in the canon mirrors the displacement of "woman" from any economy of origin and thus of originality; but it also demonstrates the extent to which the literary establishment tacitly punishes the woman who

ture. I duly removed her without so much as a whimper. I was not merely being obedient; I didn't understand the rules, I decided, and thus kept silent.

69. On this issue see, e.g., Robert D. Cottrell, "Colette's Literary Reputation," in *Women, the Arts and the 1920s in Paris and New York,* ed. Kenneth W. Wheeler and Virginia Lee Lussier (New Brunswick and London, 1982), pp. 8–13. Cottrell reminds us that Colette is missing from Germaine Brée and Margaret Guiton's 1957 *An Age of Fiction: The French Novel from Gide to Camus* (New York and Burlingame), a book which had great influence and helped shape the American understanding of the modern French canon. Colette, according to Brée and Guiton's preface, "remained aloof from the principal currents of the time." Cottrell also returns to Simone de Beauvoir's dismissal of Colette: Colette, says Beauvoir, "was after all very much engrossed in little stories about love, housekeeping and animals" (ibid., p. 12).

destabilizes the Author myth with laughter and common sense. (Colette's texts are always being questioned along the very lines which she put into doubt: Are they the Work of a great Author? Can a great author have written such lowbrow books as *Gigi?* And so on.)[70] The displacement and punishment are echoed (and aggravated) of course, by the political, legal, and everyday context in which Colette found herself. In 1900, the year *Claudine à l'école* was published, a suffragette movement was underway in France. Three feminist congresses were held that year; several feminist journals had begun (including *La Citoyenne,* whose slogan was "dare to resist"); protests and marches had taken place. The French parliament was three times presented with legislation for the rights of women—in 1901, 1906, and 1911—and three times rejected it. Divorce had become a possibility again by 1884, but only under rigorous conditions (and with a delay of three years). The law of 1804 (vigorously upheld) stated that women could choose neither a profession nor a residence without the direct approval of their husbands. Until 1893, women automatically received one-half of a man's salary for the same work, and the salary itself went directly to the husband. Not until 1900 was the working week for a woman reduced to ten hours a day; not until 1905 was a weekly day off mandatory; and not until 1907 could a woman control her own money. The vote, of course, was not to come until 1945.

In 1900, most women, including Colette, did not identify with the feminist activists, whom they thought peculiar and whose methods they found threatening. Most of the activists were women of the bourgeoisie, who were jailed, treated as outcasts, and, more to the point, perceived as idealists who believed they could do the impossible: change the legal status of women. ("Women who are free," says Claudine, "are not women.") The activists were largely pro-Dreyfus, while most husbands of the bourgeois class sported a mild anti-Semitism which they expected

70. Colette herself is far from immune to such traditional rankings. While debunking the mystique of writing, she wants to be remembered as more than the author of *Gigi* and *Chéri* (see note 45). Understandably, she wants to be acknowledged by a literary establishment on its own terms, yet free to question them.

their wives to espouse along with their other political convictions. Willy, for example, held beliefs typical of his class. As Michèle Blin Sarde puts it, he maintained an ideology of anti-Semitism, antidemocratism, nationalism, dandyism, and amoralism.[71] Indeed, Jews and women were often marginalized in the same breath. The Goncourt Academy, for example, to which Colette was later elected, had as its first motto "Pas de femmes, pas de Juifs."

* *
*

I began this chapter by pointing to the prevailing fashion of seeing modernity as rootlessness—as a site, not of origin, but of displacement, transplanting, and deterritorialization. Or, as Certeau puts it, as the impossibility of owning a place or of owning a name. But we have seen that in all of these metaphors there remains the presence of (or fiction of) an origin, a home, a first ground. These fictions are possible for a speaking subject who, as Huyssen put it, can deny his own subjectivity while taking it for granted in everyday life. But a bourgeois woman at the turn of the century in France has no real "home": neither in the domestic space to which she is relegated (since, among other things, the finances of its operation are not legally hers to control); nor in the "public" space from which she is largely barred; nor in the metaphysical discourse which constitutes her as always secondary. What for Certeau is the impossibility of ontological ground for the subject begins for a woman in Colette's situation as a legal, quotidian problem: she does not own her property under most circumstances, nor does she own her name. She cannot vote or choose her profession.

Constituted without origin and thus rootless at every level, woman (a term I use in accordance with the essentialism which produces it) is a vagabond, an immigrant *to* literature, a stranger to herself (to return to Certeau), who has, quite literally, no ground from which or on which to speak, and no discourse in

71. Sarde, *Colette*, p. 156. Willy declined to sign a petition in favor of Dreyfus, which led one wit to quip that it was the first time the famous author had refused to sign something he hadn't written.

which to engage that does not already problematize her ability to say "I."[72] Not transplanted but unplantable, she cannot be inscribed within an economy of the originary. Therefore, she will never be fully acknowledged as a genuine "Author" by the canon; nor will her efforts be seen as "work," or the "fruit of her labor" considered great literature.[73] The same logic allows, conversely, for a Willy: the essentialism underlying the romantic notion of author rests on the collective exploitation of many for the sake of the illusion of the singular genius, a living figuration of the sovereignty of the subject. One could go further and accuse any critique of the subject of titillating itself with its own demise, even as the critique itself reinforces, by virtue of its metaphysical introspection, the very subjectivity it professes to question.

Woman, then, is an ontological street person. There were many of the more literal variety in France of the 1880s, the period during which Colette was growing up and which embraced the work ethic as one way of putting the Commune behind it. Several treatises of the period denounced the street people as antibourgeois good-for-nothings, whose lolling around the streets of Paris was an insult to the good workingman's life. These drifters are seen as a class in themselves: the vagabonds. They are seen as lazy and are particularly chastised for having neither regular work, nor home, nor family. *Travaillons à nous rendre utiles* (Let us work to be useful) was one of the slogans of the day; the vagabond represents a challenge to this dictum, since he refuses to work and, perhaps equally infuriating to the work-ethic bourgoisie, wanders through Paris in an apparently aimless fashion. The vagabond does not walk to reach a destination; he wanders

72. I appreciate the irritation in Nancy Harstock's question, which is a more down-to-earth version of Huyssen's comment: "Why is it," she asks, "that just at the moment when so many of us who have been silenced begin to demand the right to name ourselves, to act as subjects rather than objects of history, that just then the concept of subjecthood becomes problematic?" "Foucault on Power: A Theory for Women?" in *Feminism/Postmodernism,* ed. Linda J. Nicholson (New York, 1990), p. 163. At the same time, it is Foucault's critique of subjectivity that allows us, to some degree, to articulate the present unimaginability of a subject position for "women," and the way such a position might eventually be constructed outside the limits of an existing (masculinist) power structure.

73. If, like George Sand or George Eliot, she is described as having the mind of a man in the body of a woman, obviously nothing has changed with regard to the status of the writing female subject.

for economic reasons, just as his imitator the *flâneur* will profess to wander for ideological ones.

La paresse, or laziness, is here a synonym for uselessness. A proclamation of independence, it is considered to be an act of defiance against the social order. It is also (and significantly) seen as the male version of loose morals in a woman. One functionary of the period snorts, "Vagabondage is for the apprentice what prostitution is for the young woman worker."[74] Here the attempt is to feminize (and therefore neutralize the radicality of) vagabondage, a tactic I shall discuss in the following chapter.

Equally to the point, however, is the feminine side of the equation: the woman who falls into prostitution is not doing real work. During the same period in Paris, P. C. H. Brouardel, a forensic pathologist much admired by Freud, is purported to have said, "Dirty knees are the sign of an honest girl."[75]

Prostitutes also wander—they are streetwalkers. Theirs is another form of vagabondage, then, of apparently aimless cruising. With both the vagabond and the prostitute, the moral outrage professes to focus on the dispersed, aleatoric aspect they display. The prostitute wanders at will between sexual partners. Her economy announces itself to be freely disseminated—the obverse of a goal-oriented work ethic. Even more scandalous is the profitability of the prostitute's wanderings. Beneath the outrage at the loitering of both vagabond and prostitute lies a recognition of the threat these two "types" present. For both fly in the face of, laugh at, the bourgeois work ethic and the moralism it wants to present as irrefutable. Theodore Homberg, in a book published in 1880, called vagabonds "the most dangerous enemies of soci-

74. Cited in Ross, *The Emergence of Social Space*, p. 57. Ross has an excellent discussion of the vagabond in Baudelaire's Paris.

75. When Freud was a student of Charcot, in Paris (1885), he admired Brouardel's lectures and postmortems. "On one occasion," writes Freud, Brouardel was discussing "the indications which enabled one to judge the social rank, character, and origin of an unidentified body. And I heard him say, 'Les genoux sales sont le signe d'une fille honnête.' He was using a girl's dirty knees as evidence of her virtue." Men on the other hand, adds Freud, are embarrassed by their animal origins, and try to wash them away. Preface to the German translation of J. G. Bourke's *Scatalogic Rites of All Nations* (1891). *Standard Edition*, vol. 12, p. 335. For an excellent series of articles on the gendering of work, see *On Work: Historical, Comparative and Theoretical Approaches*, ed. R. E. Pahl (Oxford and New York, 1988).

ety." He then arrives at the real concern: "The vagabond, having nothing to lose in moments of social upheaval, desires such moments and helps out in the hopes of gaining something."[76]

When Colette chooses to write a largely autobiographical work entitled *La Vagabonde,* the various resonances of that work must be understood in their context. The novel itself is as "loose" as its title: it was published not as a unified piece but as a serial in the popular magazine *La Vie Parisienne,* between May 21 and October 1 of 1910. It announced itself as one of the popular novels which dominated the journals of the period. The title of the novel boldly coins the feminine version of the vagabond, and is thus willfully, doubly scandalous. Colette's title insists upon the rootless, wandering quality of a woman in her position: a divorced woman without means in belle époque France is exploited as a laborer unless she succumbs to scandalous modes of living (which, of course, entail a different type of exploitation). *La Vagabonde* tells of Colette's own "checkered" life: her need to turn to the music hall and the theater for a living when her husband left her, and her sudden exuberance at discovering her independence, her enjoyment. The same bourgeois ethic that condemns the women of the music hall had made it impossible for Colette to earn a living as a writer once Willy divorced her. She had no name as a writer, no reputation upon which to play, and no rights to her own previous writings.

La Vagabonde writes of the freedom which can be found for the displaced. I read *La Vagabonde* as more than a cry of liberation from Willy's iron hand; as more than what Michèle Sarde calls "a hymn to freedom." *La Vagabonde* embraces the status of the divorced woman as marginal and turns the state of the displaced into the condition for freedom. As such, the novel is not only a highly disruptive text; it is also a modernist one, promoting rootlessness (but for reasons different than those of a Guattari, a Deleuze, or a Certeau) as a condition to be cultivated rather than avoided for the female subject.

---

76. From Theodore Homberg's *Etude sur le vagabondage* (Paris, 1880). Cited by Ross, p. 58. See also Homberg's contemporary, Gustave Le Bon, *La psychologie des foules* (1895), translated as *The Crowd* (Harmondsworth, U.K., 1981). Huyssen argues that fear of the crowd is fear of women.

The extent to which, in bourgeois ideology, streetwalking is the purview only of a woman, and the degree to which vagabondage and streetpeople are necessarily rejected by the same ideology, will be taken up in the next chapter. As against the ethic of work, goal-oriented striding, and what is perceived as masculine, there emerges the assumed triad of wandering (cruising, streetwalking), laziness, and "femininity." To this peculiar logic we now turn again: this time, in the figure and writings of Walter Benjamin.

4

Walter Benjamin and
the Right to Acedia

Work itself puts in a word. And writing about work makes
up part of the skill necessary to perform it.

BENJAMIN, "The Author as Producer"

Sloth [is] a kind of sorrow because sorrow is not a distinct
vice, in so far as a man shirks a distasteful and burdensome
work, or sorrows on account of any other cause whatever,
but only in so far as he is sorry on account of the Divine
good, which sorrow belongs essentially to sloth; since sloth
seeks undue rest in so far as it spurns the Divine good.

AQUINAS, *Summa Theologica*

Yet the productive life is the life of the species.

MARX, *Economic and Philosophic Manuscripts of 1844*

FOR THE CONSERVATIVE social reformers of the 1920s and
1930s, the flâneur is not much better than the vagabond,
whom he both precedes and supersedes. The flâneur is parasitic on a productive society, one to which he neither belongs
nor (worse still) wishes to belong. He has no routine, no recognizable everyday life, although daily life is what he observes the
most; he does not work and, significantly, does not buy into the
work ethic. Even the dictionary definition of the French word is
possessed of a moralizing tone: the flâneur, says the *Petit Robert*,
is someone who *enjoys* doing nothing ("qui aime à ne rien faire");
the word *work* is given as the antonym. According to the Larousse, the verb *flâner* means to wander about aimlessly with fre-

quent stops for looking; to waste time ("Errer sans but, en s'arrê-
tant souvent pour regarder. Perdre son temps"). It would be
difficult to deny that these definitions, whose ostensible purpose
is to impart information "objectively," are heavily laden with the
vocabulary of a work ethic ideology. For the *Robert* (which gives
a less loaded definition), enjoying doing nothing is the opposite
of work. The flâneur and work are irreconcilable notions, an-
tonyms at the conceptual as well as the syntactic level. The Larousse is more explicit: to wander without a goal, to interrupt
one's gait for the purpose of looking, is the same as wasting one's
time. This rhetoric of utilitarianism, of valorizing work as against
strolling and gazing, and, more importantly, of seeing the flâneur
as antithetical to work, contains the crux of a problem to be dealt
with here: we are back to the politics of laziness.

The extent to which the work ethic permeates every aspect
of social behavior and analysis in "modern" (that is, nineteenth-
century) capitalism has, of course, been amply demonstrated. As
Max Weber pointed out, modern capitalist society necessitates a
disciplined labor force because its goal is economic efficiency.
Thus "man is dominated by the making of money, by acquisition
as the ultimate purpose of his life." But this goal-oriented modus
vivendi carries with it the rejection of enjoyment: "The *summa
bonum* of this ethic," says Weber, "the earning of more and more
money," is combined with "the strict avoidance of all spontaneous enjoyment of life." It is above all "completely devoid of any
eudaemonistic, not to say hedonistic, admixture." Added to the
capitalist rejection of enjoyment is what Weber calls "certain religious ideas." He quotes Benjamin Franklin's own quotation from
the Bible ("drummed into him again and again," says Weber, by
his strict Calvinist father): "Seest thou a man diligent in his business? he shall stand before kings" (Proverbs 22:29).[1]

The spirit of modern capitalism (in Weber's sense—Western
European and American), by insisting upon efficiency and the
reinvestment of capital, produces a moral code which turns to
Calvinist principles for religious resonance. My point here, which

---

1. Max Weber, *The Protestant Ethic and the Spirit of Capitalism* (New York, 1976),
p. 53.

has motivated my rehearsal of Weber's well-known argument, is that the capitalist work ethic as Weber articulates it in 1904 entails more than an insistence upon goal-oriented living and upon money for its own sake. It also preaches a simultaneous devalorization of "hedonism"—and of eudaemonism, in itself an ethical system which judges moral action by its ability to create happiness. It is not just that work becomes, in "modern capitalism," the sine qua non of the man of the street; more convolutedly and more insidiously, pleasure becomes a kind of moral flabbiness unless it is inscribed in the "leisure" hours dictated by the work place (the corollary assumption here is that to refuse to participate in the work force is to indulge in pleasure). The subtext is the maintenance of capitalism, the ideology of which the flâneur scorns by his very presence on the streets as loiterer, by his aimless strolling during working hours, by his exhibitionistic "wasting" of valuable time. He is a streetperson, not a "man on the street," regardless of his actual politics. He is a fly in the ointment, a scandal. It is in this sense that the flâneur is as ominous as was the vagabond for Theodore Homberg.

Homberg, it will be recalled, thought the vagabond was the "most dangerous" enemy of society because he had nothing to lose. The vagabond "desires" moments of "social upheaval" and even helps out "in the hopes of gaining something." While the flâneur, unlike the vagabond, frequently has the means to loiter, and has acquired the luxuries offered by this same brand of capitalism, he is no less disruptive of its "spirit" than is his poorer brother. They are both streetpeople, flaunting their idleness in the face of a work-oriented society. They both go against the grain of the urban crowd. The flâneur, like the vagabond, interrupts the flow of busy humanity on the city streets. Both rupture the efficiency of the pedestrian; they even disrupt the linearity of movement (which is in itself an extension of the smooth progress of the production line). In the case of the flâneur, it is not just that he offends by not working; he also observes in a nonlinear fashion, one which uses collage, pastiche, interruption, the aleatoric—the converse of the linear and the efficient—as modes of seeing to be constantly cultivated. He accumulates not wealth but fleeting, disconnected moments, which he will paste together; he is a conceptual *chiffonier* (ragpicker), as Benjamin was to put it. In his ability to lounge, the flâneur is the living product of the same capitalist class system that his activities openly reject.

The flâneur, then, is viewed in terms of the leisure/work dichotomy, which he both threatens and to a certain degree exploits. That dichotomy is clearly a product of an Enlightenment bourgeois mentality. In Marxian theory, however, the dichotomy is also firmly in place, even if the agenda is (obviously) different. Lukács, for example, reads Diderot's *Le neveu de Rameau* (which presents an earlier prototype for the flâneur) as an instance where bourgeois ideals are dissolved "by their own economic basis, by the forces of capitalism." Like Engels, Lukács sees *Rameau's Nephew* as a "precursor of dialectical materialism."[2] Engels and Lukács use Diderot's text to demonstrate the leisure/work dichotomy as the capitalist legacy; but they fail to question the categories or implications of that dichotomy. We will see that such an elision, such an acceptance of the leisure/work split inside a Marxist critique, extends beyond Engels and Lukács. It entails the absorption of the work ethic into certain kinds of critiques—critiques inimical to the Calvinistic and work-code morality underpinning "modern capitalism."

Adherence to the leisure/work dichotomy brings with it the language and ideology of gendering. Leisure, as we noted in the last chapter, is aligned not only with laziness but with the "feminine," whereas work becomes aligned with a virilized proletariat. With these notions in mind, then, let us see what happens when Hannah Arendt and Theodor Adorno try to present the texts of their dead friend, Walter Benjamin, to an American public in the 1950s.

The problem begins with the desire to be taken seriously. Benjamin had wanted to be the best literary critic in Germany, but felt that for the fifty previous years criticism had no longer been considered a serious genre (*genre sérieux*) in Germany. The only solution, he felt, was to move to Paris and to recreate criticism as

---

2. Georg Lukács, *Studies in European Realism* (New York: Grosset and Dunlap, 1964), pp. 76 and 103. He even echoes Engel's phrase "masterpiece of dialectic" to describe the book (p. 106). Both, of course, are largely following Hegel's reading of the same text.

a genre—to make it serious again, in other words.[3] This double marginalization—the choice of living not-at-home and of focusing on what is largely perceived as a peripheral discourse—is a commonplace in Benjamin studies, but I use it here to contextualize the tenor of his two early interpreters and introducers.

Hannah Arendt, in her introduction to the American collection of Benjamin's essays (which she called *Illuminations*), points to the importance of metaphor in Benjamin's work. Metaphor, she explains, must be taken in the sense of "transfer," (*metaphērein*) and, above all, as nonallegorical. Whereas allegory entails the solving of a riddle, she adds, metaphor "has borne that element of the poetic which conveys cognition; its use establishes the *correspondences* between physically most remote things." In a tone resonating (consciously, I assume) with Heidegger, she writes: "Metaphors are the means by which the oneness of the world is poetically brought about. What is so hard to understand about Benjamin is that without being a poet he *thought poetically* and therefore was bound to regard the metaphor as the greatest gift of language" (14–15). The result of this poetic dwelling of thought in Benjamin is, Arendt argues, a fascination on his part with what "others" brand as "'vulgar-Marxist' or 'undialectical' thinking." This syllogism is bizarre: it assumes that the insistence on metaphor allows Benjamin the easy move from the superstructure to "sensually experienced data" (the material substructure)—a move which is promptly mimed by Arendt in the very articulation of its possibility.

Arendt's insistence on metaphor as the dominant trait ("since Homer") of poetry is debatable. (She seems to conflate it with simile at certain times and with analogical thinking at others.) More to the point, her introduction ultimately serves to put Benjamin at risk, largely on grounds of his "seriousness" and, as an apparent (albeit tacit) corollary, of his originality. Noting that Benjamin chose to move in with his parents rather than to work, Arendt contends that even though this situation was intolerable for him, "he never *seriously* considered another solution" (25). She says that despite "permanent financial trouble" he managed

3. Arendt, *Illuminations* (New York, 1969), p. 23.

"constantly to enlarge his library" and adds, with obvious disapproval, that this constitutes "an expensive passion." She reminds us that Benjamin found his father's insistence that he work "unspeakable"; that the only "gainful employment" the son would consider was opening a secondhand bookshop but that "nothing came of it, of course." It is the "of course" that is of interest here.

Arendt joins Max Rychner in eliding the pace of Benjamin's thinking with his gait, and both with the stroll of the flâneur. She explains it as largely a result of class: Benjamin, like the flâneur, had his home in the nineteenth century, an age of security in which children of upper-middle-class families were assured of an income without having to work, so that they had no reason to "hurry" (22).[4] Benjamin, then, is not-at-home because of era rather than geography, although the latter plays a role in the exile. Because Paris "invites" *flânerie,* it "naturally aroused in him a feeling for French literature as well, and this almost irrevocably estranged him from normal German intellectual life."

The thrust of Arendt's introduction is to impress upon the American reader the fact that Benjamin is a foreigner to "normal German intellectual life." This seems to mean, not only that he never worked except when he had to, but also that even when he did "work" he produced very little (he would have preferred the aphorism "if he had not been paid by the line"); that he liked French literature because he had perhaps too long strolled in the streets of Paris; that he suffered from a secular version of the "ancient Jewish belief that those who 'learn' . . . were the true elite of the people and should not be bothered with so vulgar an occupation as making money or working for it" (26). Arendt ends by reminding her readers that Kafka, "possibly because he really was something like a genius," never claimed to be one and took an "ordinary job at the Prague Workmen's compensation office" (26).

---

4. As Roland Barthes notes, the French word for laziness, *paresse,* is related to the Latin *piger* (slow), so that the slow pace of sloth is in the etymology. "Dare to Be Lazy," *The Grain of the Voice: Interviews 1962–1980,* trans. Linda Coverdale (New York, 1985). In *The Protestant Ethic,* Weber has a series of footnotes on sloth. "Sloth and idleness," he writes, paraphrasing the Puritan legacy, "are such deadly sins because they have a cumulative character" (p. 264). They are the antithesis of the methodical life.

It would take a long time to unpack all of the extraordinary
claims Arendt makes in her introduction, and even longer to assess those claims and the barely controlled irritation inspiring
them. But we can extract a few claims of our own here: Arendt
recalls that the flâneur has his ancestry in the nineteenth century,
and in the dandy in particular. She explains Benjamin's writing
in terms of the flâneur's gait and indolence; she distances herself
from him as an intellectual German Jew (which she is as well)
on grounds that he became enamored of French literature rather
than taking up the "normal" interests of German intellectuals
(which, one can assume, are more *serious*—that is, political and
philosophical rather than literary); that he is representative of an
entire generation of sons of successful Jewish businessmen
"whose dream it was that their sons were destined for higher
things."

Arendt suggests that Benjamin may have produced so little
precisely because he was an *homme de lettres.* His library, which he
lived with, was "by no means intended as a *working tool*" (my
emphasis) since Benjamin collected but did not read most of the
books. Arendt describes the library as "guaranteed not to be useful or at the service of any profession" (23). And she adds, "Such
an existence was something unknown in Germany." It is on these
grounds, then, that Benjamin deviates from "normal German intellectual life": he is representative of the upper class in general,
which is unable to validate work and its twin partners, production and utility. He collects things as *objets,* not as tools.

The Arendt essay succeeds in articulating Benjamin's exile on
grounds, not that he was a Jewish refugee, but that he did not
apply the work ethic to his intellectual projects; that he was literary (French) rather than philosophical/political (German). His
projects are seen as contaminated by this indolence, just as surely
as Paris explains why he slowed his gait. From her New York
apartment filled with books which she uses as tools, Arendt condemns Benjamin for his laziness: it is French and not German; it
is the privilege of the male Jewish scholar gone secular. In short,
Benjamin did not fulfill his dream of creating a new genre, says
Arendt, and "the very notion of thus becoming a useful member
of society would have repelled him." He can only be described

as an author by means of "a great many negative statements" (presumably Arendt means negative remarks of which she is aware; she lists comments such as "His erudition was great, but he was no scholar"). Benjamin's importance and place as "author," then, are subject to doubt because, unlike the true "genius" Kafka, he would not take an ordinary job, would not value production, would not hurry, and thus would not admit to the value of time. These are the "negatives" that must be invoked if we are to include Benjamin's work and person "as an author within our usual framework of reference" (3).

Arendt's tone and assumptions would be little more than a curiosity were they not seconded (even more shrilly) by Adorno. He too elides the writing with the life of Benjamin. It should be noted, however, that Benjamin himself seems to encourage, to some extent, this type of biographical judgment. His acknowledged debt to Baudelaire and Proust, for example, is motivated not only by the fact that they were both famous dandies, but also by Baudelaire's overwhelming sense of *ennui* (or spleen) and descriptions of its debilitating effects, and Proust's outright withdrawal into a hermetic immobilization with a concomitant scrutiny of memory as a means, not so much of recapturing, but of expressing what is lost. Thus Benjamin's essays themselves make the move of conflating biography and text.[5] Nevertheless, the moralizing and judgmental character of Adorno's vocabulary in his Benjamin studies reads like a kind of modern summa theologicae on the evils of sloth.

Adorno's essays on Benjamin appeal consistently to metaphor, the overriding one being Benjamin's own, the "dialectic at a standstill." This trope of the standstill is one which Adorno's essays will insist and embroider upon, thus implying that the personal paralysis (which includes the inability to hold down a steady job) is mirrored in a kind of nonprogression or quicksand in the thought. In "A Portrait of Walter Benjamin," Adorno de-

5. And then there is Benjamin's autobiographical text, *Berliner Kindheit um Neunzehnhundert* (Frankfurt a.M., 1977). Also the essay "The Destructive Character," largely regarded as autobiographical (in *Reflections: Walter Benjamin,* ed. Peter Demetz ([New York, 1978], pp. 301–3). But these are merely two of the more obvious examples; all of Benjamin is auto-referential, including his tendency toward self-citation.

scribes his subject as neither "vital" nor "organic."[6] The elements of civilization to which he is drawn are "petrified, frozen, or obsolete." More serious still, "the glance of his philosophy is Medusan": he liked glass balls with frozen landscapes, and "*nature morte* could be written above the portals of his philosophical dungeons." In short, Adorno sees everything that Benjamin touches as rendered static, and characterizes his friend (his "mentor" as the *New York Times Book Review* is quoted as saying on the back of *Prisms*) as possessing an intellectual energy reminiscent of mental atomic fission, dissolving the insoluble and grasping the essentials. The implosive quality of this metaphor notwithstanding, Adorno still casts Benjamin's thought in terms of a kind of cognitive freeze tag.

Benjamin reminds Adorno of the Christmas tree which children love to peek at on Christmas eve, yet which (and here Adorno waxes Proustian himself) promises more than it can deliver: "But the light, as one of reason, also promised truth itself, not its powerless shadow" (*Prisms,* 230). Finally, in a move that doubles Arendt's negative definition of Benjamin, Adorno comments that for Benjamin "the metaphor of the creator is thoroughly inappropriate" (229) because Benjamin's "own contribution to his work was not anything 'vital' or 'organic,'" and because Benjamin "had nothing of the philosopher in him."[7]

Despite Adorno's politically correct demurring (that the notion of "creator" is nothing more than a rhetorical figure, and is inap-

6. In *Prisms* (Cambridge, MA, 1990), p. 233. As Michael W. Jennings notes, Adorno had been an early admirer and interpreter of Benjamin, offering a seminar at Frankfurt on the *Trauerspiel* shortly after it had been rejected as a thesis for *Habilitation* there. Jennings adds, "By the late 1930s, however, Adorno's own intellectual accomplishments led to a change in tone and a perhaps necessary denial of Benjamin's influence on his thought. His criticism—and his failure to include the essay in the 1955 edition of Benjamin's selected works—has had a remarkable effect on its reception." *Dialectical Images: Walter Benjamin's Theory of Literary Criticism* (Ithaca, NY, 1987) p. 30, n. 19. For the complete writings of Adorno on Benjamin, see *Über Walter Benjamin* (Frankfurt, a.M., 1970).

7. Lest the many experts who constitute the great architecture of the Benjamin industry be concerned that I am doing Arendt and Adorno an injustice in my reading of their Benjamin sketches, let me say that it is more than evident how and why they admired him. What remains less obvious is what they found intolerable and on what grounds. It is also important to my argument here to see how the rhetoric of Arendt and Adorno might betray certain assumptions—assumptions that have framed my own in the development of the present study.

plicable to Benjamin on rhetorical grounds, as a metaphor), or Arendt's similar gesture, which claims that Benjamin cannot be called an author "within our usual framework of reference," both texts hold up "normal German intellectual life" as a standard that includes the very validation these assessments of Benjamin profess to rise above. Despite their belittling of claims of author or creator (or, let us recall, "scholar," "genius," and other such terms), by denying Benjamin access to such claims, the texts of Arendt and Adorno virtually condemn him to a position as eccentric recorder of the times, or intelligent dilettante who was onto something in spite of himself. What emerges from the language of Arendt and Adorno is that Benjamin's project was as much nonwork and nonutilitarian as was his life. They both seem shocked by Benjamin's rise to prominence: "Posthumous fame is too odd a thing to be blamed upon the blindness of the world or the corruption of a literary milieu," writes Arendt, and concludes that it belongs, as it does with Benjamin, to "the unclassifiable ones." But although she claims that everything Benjamin wrote was sui generis, it turns out that the "unclassifiable" writers neither fit the old order "nor introduced a new genre that can be classified." They remain, in other words, incomprehensible—a fate that Arendt would never have wished for herself.

The same moves, grounded in a perhaps unconscious *recusatio* (we are, after all, looking at rhetoric) are to be found in Adorno. What does it mean when Adorno begins his "Portrait of Walter Benjamin" with the following bizarre assessment? "The name of the philosopher who took his life while fleeing Hitler's executioners has, in the more than twenty years since then, acquired a certain nimbus, despite the esoteric character of his early writings and the fragmentary nature of his later ones" (229). Bizarre because he neither names nor acknowledges Benjamin's achievements—indeed, he almost attempts to erase them. In a text professing to deride the significance of original creation, there is too much overdetermined nonchalance in the phrase "acquired a certain nimbus" for the reader to remain unsuspicious. So too, Arendt's text dismisses the usual "framework" of the notion "author" even as she removes any hope for a claim on the term by Benjamin, and remains bemused at the thought of his "posthumous fame" (which she depersonalizes as simply an "odd" event in general).

In another essay that characterizes Benjamin, Adorno's metaphors are similarly drawn from those of his subject, and similarly reliant on the theme of the static. "Constellation," "cristallization," and "force field" are the figures Adorno uses here.[8] Certain figures return from the other essay: the "petrified," the "medusan, fixating gaze" (11), the dialectic at a standstill, the notion of concentrating on the minute ("in which historical movement halts and sediments into an image"). Benjamin makes himself into the "seismograph of the moment" (15), and he is again like a Christmas tree "seen when the door is cracked open to the living room and an overwhelming flood of light fills the eyes with tears" (17). It is a light more "shattering and certain" than any seen directly "when one is finally called to enter the room."

The Christmas tree metaphor (which, among other things, suggests how important a holiday this was for Adorno and reminds us that Benjamin himself wrote on Christmas trees) means something much more complicated than simply that Benjamin promises more than he can deliver, although that is certainly one indirect connotation. In such instants, Adorno writes, the whole of Benjamin's thought was assembled, "and to them alone has passed what theological doctrines once promised" (16). The shattering light of anticipation, of prisms crossing and crisscrossing into constellations, seem to give a hope of unity of past and present, of centers in peripheries, of Proustian *moments privilégiés*. It is perhaps also, however, a metaphor of the hope of assimilation, of the moment of happiness which eases what Adorno calls sadness. Adorno links sadness in Benjamin directly to his "nature," but also to "Jewish awareness of the permanence of danger and catastrophe," as well as to the antiquarian tendency to "see the present transformed into the ancient past, as if by enchantment" (15). While Benjamin may have been "productive" at every moment of his waking life, he had a "preponderance of spirit" which

8. Adorno, "Introduction to Benjamin's *Schriften*," in *On Walter Benjamin: Critical Essays and Recollections,* ed. Gary Smith (Cambridge, MA, 1988), pp. 2–17. Originally published in Walter Benjamin, *Schriften,* ed. Theodor W. Adorno and Gretel Adorno in collaboration with Friedrich Podszus (Frankfurt a.M., 1955).

"radically alienated him from his physical and even his psychological existence." This alienation, Adorno suggests, lies at the origin of Benjamin's sadness and melancholy.

The Christmas tree metaphor, then, reminds us of the alienation of Benjamin as a Jew from the culture he flees; at the same time, it is a metaphor which, assimilated as it is into Adorno's discourse as a marker of (his own?) childhood memories, serves to return Adorno to the center of that culture while keeping Benjamin at its periphery and at the margins of political thought. For Adorno, Benjamin has the sadness of the Jews, a sadness linked to the nostalgia for the past, that "antiquarian tendency."

Benjamin himself speaks of this sadness, and in a manner indirectly connected with theology: it is acedia, the deadly sin of sloth. In one of his theses on the philosophy of history, Benjamin describes acedia as that from which historical materialism distances itself, "a process of empathy whose origin is in the indolence of the heart, *acedia,* which despairs of grasping and holding the genuine historical image as it flares up briefly. Among medieval theologians it was regarded as the root cause of sadness. Flaubert, who was familiar with it, wrote, 'Peu de gens devineront combien il a fallu être triste pour ressusciter Carthage.'"[9] For Benjamin, acedia is a problem of a relation to history; it is partially related to Proust's involuntary memory, or to Baudelaire's *correspondance.* It is the ability to extract the whole from the particular and, more importantly, to retrieve the past by superimposing it on the present, not by representing the present as the culmination, or aggregate, of a past narrative ("history breaks down into images, not into stories"). In Proust as in Baudelaire, the present has moments when it "flares up briefly" almost as an epiphany (the uneven stones at the end of *La Recherche,* or the brief meeting of the eyes in Baudelaire's "A une Passante"). These

---

9. *Illuminations,* p. 256. Demetz notes that Benjamin's notion of *Rettung* (redemption) should not be overlooked as a contrast, if not antidote, to the melancholy which permeates his texts: "For all his pessimism, Benjamin remained convinced that a revolutionary potential lay buried in the ruins of nineteenth-century bourgeois life." *Reflections,* pp. 37–38. On Benjamin's idea of *Rettung,* see the unsurpassed article by Jürgen Habermas, "Consciousness-Raising or Redemptive Criticism: The Contemporaneity of Walter Benjamin," trans. Phillip Brewster and Carl H. Büchner, in *New German Critique* 17 (Spring 1979): 30–59.

moments are privileged *because* they are indicative of what will never be, or will never be again. Hence spleen for Baudelaire and the indolence of the bedridden Proust.

Sadness for Benjamin is in this same tradition of the moment with the recognition of loss superimposed upon it: "Few will be able to guess how sad one had to be in order to resuscitate Carthage." A belief that the past can be resuscitated is the attitude of the historian. Historicism empathizes with the victors of history: "Historical materialists know what that means. Whoever has emerged victorious participates to this day in the triumphal procession in which the present rulers step over those who are lying prostrate" (*Illuminations*, 256). Benjamin's sadness springs from the thought that history belongs to the victors; their spoils are called "cultural treasures." For him, acedia presents the gaze of the "historical materialist," of his dilemma. It is not the scandal of sloth; it is tied to the interruptive notion of memory.

If we look at the way acedia is described by the Church theologians, however, we discover that the vocabulary is strangely reminiscent of our secular dictionaries, with whose definitions on the flâneur we began this chapter. For Aquinas, sloth is sin because it impedes the performance of one's duties, and entails a willful shutting out of divine goodness.[10] As he puts it in the passage quoted at the opening of this chapter, acedia is a kind of sorrow; it entails the shirking of work and the seeking of "undue rest."

10. ". . . because the proper effect of charity is joy in God . . . while sloth is sorrow about spiritual good in as much as it is a Divine good." *Summa Theologicae*, art. 3. Although there was an attempt to demote acedia from sin to vice (e.g. St. Gregory in the eighth century) by emphasizing the sadness as above the evils of sloth, acedia remained a sin, even if the qualities for which it was noted shifted in stress. The *Catholic Encyclopedia of Religion* says that acedia is a disgust with the spiritual "because of the physical effort involved" (p. 81). Thus Adorno's notion of the alienation in Benjamin is as if mirrored in this definition, which goes on to note that acedia is the plight of the lonely (e.g. the hermit) and can manifest itself not only as laziness, but (according to John Cassian's *On the Spirit of Acedia*) "even in nervous activity." For the history of the development of the concept, see A. L. Huxley, "Accidie," in *On the Margin* (London, 1923). See also E. Waugh, "Sloth," in *The Seven Deadly Sins*, ed. I. Fleming (New York, 1962). Finally, for the history of the concept and the ways in which it remains a sin rather than the mere vice of melancholy, there is the classic work by Siegfried Wenzel, *The Sin of Sloth: Acedia in Medieval Thought and Literature* (Chapel Hill, NC, 1967). I am most grateful to Donald Pearce for helping me to clarify my ideas on acedia.

Moreover, acedia has "six daughter sins": faintheartedness, wandering (of the mind), sluggishness, spite, despair (or melancholy), and malice. Thus acedia, itself a feminine name, is further gendered (as are all cardinal sins: "a capital sin is one to which daughters are assigned") by having "daughters." It is a feminized sin in view, one might imagine, of its lack of linearity (wanderings); its weaknesses (faintheartedness, sluggishness, despair); and its shrewish qualities (spite and malice).[11] Of these "daughter sins," only the last, spite and malice, are not immediately and insistently attributed to Benjamin in the texts we have been considering here. The theological text allows us to extract the insidious gendering of laziness to which we have referred throughout this study. It also, I think, permits us to claim that in conflating Benjamin's slothful life with his wandering texts, Adorno and Arendt subtly feminize both him and his writing, a gendering which, given the dominant masculinist culture, cannot fail to have its (negative) effects.

Returning to Adorno's metaphor that "the glance of [Benjamin's] philosophy is Medusan," or that his is a "Medusan, fixating gaze," we now see that it participates in this strange convergence of tropes which force a feminization (in the sense of misogynistic play of stereotyping) of Benjamin and his project. According to Freud, after all, the Medusa's head represents a woman "as a being who frightens and repels because she is castrated."[12] In a

11. As Juliana Schiesari points out, women have been systematically excluded from what she calls the canon of melancholia. *The Gendering of Melancholia: Feminism, Psychoanalysis, and the Symbolics of Loss in Renaissance Literature* (Ithaca, NY, 1992). She cites, for example, the classic *Saturn and Melancholia,* ed. Raymond Klibansky, Erwin Panofsky, and Fritz Saxl (New York, 1964). This is an exhaustive study which never places women in any direct way within the economy of melancholy.

12. Freud, "Medusa's Head," *Standard Edition,* 18:273–74. See also Neil Hertz, "Medusa's Head: Male Hysteria under Political Pressure," in *The End of the Line* (New York, 1985), pp. 161–82. Tasso uses the figure of the Hydra (which is related to the Medusa) as a metaphor of the excess of thought plaguing melancholics. See *Gerusalemme liberata,* ed. Fredi Chiapelli (Milan, 1982), pp. iv, 4–8. Such an excess is one of the problems Adorno sees in Benjamin. Adorno quotes Benjamin quoting Goethe: they are both, for Adorno, the Chancery clerks of their own interior. As Schiesari reminds us, Burton also ties the Hydra/Medusa to melancholy: he begins his *Anatomy of Melancholy* with the figure of the Hydra as a metaphor of endless dispute. Such a figure might find its modern manifestation in the Benjamin critical industry, of which Adorno and Arendt are merely the tip of the iceberg, to continue the static metaphors.

strange and certainly unacknowledged (and unconscious) way, the tone and rhetoric of Adorno's and Arendt's introductory essays and thumbnail sketches of Benjamin subtly castrate his importance by casting his style and life in feminized tropes, and by taking their distance. It is in this light that I am reading the sentence by Adorno cited earlier: "The name of the philosopher who took his life while fleeing executioners has . . . acquired a certain nimbus, despite . . ."

Adorno and Arendt, when they go about characterizing Benjamin, are far from alone in their articulation of sadness as inherent to sloth (or vice versa), or in their description of a life which parallels the work (in its fragmentary, wandering quality, or in its melancholic laziness), or finally, in their recourse to a misogynist economy to underpin all of these.

Some or all of such constructs are to be found in a good deal of Benjamin criticism. The early Fredric Jameson, for example, sees Benjamin as being principally motivated by nostalgia, and concludes that he is possessed of an allegorical, not really a Marxist thought. (The first part of this assessment is almost exactly what Benjamin says about Baudelaire—that his melancholy makes his genius an allegorical one. But for Benjamin, this is unimpugned praise.) After mentioning the "hysterical heroes of Poe and Baudelaire," Jameson adds, "Benjamin is himself foremost among these depressed and hyperconscious visionaries who people his pages." But Jameson gets accused of acedia himself, and on nationalist (so to speak), academic grounds. Peter Demetz sees Jameson's take on Benjamin as not only one which agrees with Adorno but as in itself fundamentally melancholic: Jameson's essay, Demetz writes, "fully supports Adorno's claims and adds a dash of inevitable melancholy characteristic of American academic Marxists in their frustrating search for an old-fashioned proletariat."[13] Melancholy becomes a virus to which each Benja-

13. Fredric Jameson, *Marxism and Form* (Princeton, 1971), p. 71. Demetz, *Reflections,* p. viii. In *The Political Unconscious* (Ithaca, NY, 1981), Jameson lines Benjamin (especially the Baudelaire essay) up with the mechanistic Marxist tradition; what Jameson calls "billiard ball causality" (p. 25). Michael W. Jennings will see this as a wrong read as well; *Dialectical Images: Walter Benjamin's Theory of Literary Criticism* (Ithaca, NY, 1987) p. 34.

min scholar can accuse another of succumbing. There is also, for example, Jauss, who faults Benjamin's Baudelaire for being too negative, thus losing the "productive" aspect of the *Fleurs du mal*. Here the vocabulary shows its hand: sadness erodes the productive, even the valorization of the *vita activa*—in Arendt's sense (and not coincidentally): labor, work, and action.[14]

Gershom Scholem and Pierre Missac—disparate as they may be—separately (and affectionately) fault Benjamin for an unsystematic thought, for wavering, for flâneries of the mind. Missac opens his contribution to Gary Smith's collection *On Walter Benjamin* by referring in the same breath to the "complexity of Benjamin's personality" and the difficulty of classifying his *oeuvre*.[15] The result, he adds, is that scholars portray Benjamin as either sitting between two stools (*zwischen den Stühlen*) or as oscillating "between atheism and theology" (*Benjamin*, 212). Because Benjamin defies classification, his texts generate critical readings which themselves take exception to the oscillation (Benjamin is for them maddeningly inconsistent) or choose one pole over the other, insisting on dichotomies and thereby missing the subtleties of his thought; he is either "Manichean" or a "Marxist rabbi" (ibid.). The editor's note assures us that Missac's is "a unique voice of an *homme de lettres* (as Hannah Arendt described Benjamin), moving intelligently between Benjamin's life and works" (ibid., 210). This is a move made by the editor himself, since the collection is subtitled *Critical Essays and Recollections*. Scholem, who sees theological elements in Benjamin's thought and thinks Benjamin's turn to Marx undermined his creativity, speaks of the famous angel of history as "basically a melancholy figure." Combining his own insistence on Benjamin as theological with a "So

14. Hans Robert Jauss, "Nachtrag (zu dem Kapitel: 'Die Moderne' in Walter Benjamins Baudelaire-Fragmenten)," in *Literaturgeschichte als Provokation* (Frankfurt, a.M., 1970), pp. 57–66 (unavailable, to my knowledge, in English); Hannah Arendt, *The Human Condition* (Chicago, 1958).

15. Pierre Missac, "Walter Benjamin: From Rupture to Shipwreck," in Smith, *On Walter Benjamin*, p. 211. Missac, who has translated Benjamin and presented his work to the French reading public, has also written an account of the conspiracy of which some Benjamin scholars were accused in the late 1960s in Germany. See Missac, "Du Nouveau sur Walter Benjamin," *Critique*, August–September 1969, 267–68.

there!" type of scholarly rectitude, Scholem tells us in a footnote that Benjamin read "very little" Marx apart from "The Eighteenth Brumaire."[16]

Then there are all the critical essays examining Benjamin's lack of professionalism (which is another way of reminding us that he never really "worked"), most of which center on the failed *Habilitation* thesis, *The Origin of German Trauerspiel.* I shall only mention two such essays, those of Stanley Mitchel and Irving Wohlfarth. Mitchel's introduction to the English version of *Versuche über Brecht* echoes Arendt, noting that "Benjamin's idiosyncratic and difficult cast of mind blocked his way to an academic career."[17] "Barred from secure employment," he adds, Benjamin "became an itinerant man of letters." Had Benjamin earned an academic post, he muses, "it is difficult to say how his thought would have developed." Wohlfarth reads Benjamin's initially unpublished preface to *The Trauerspiel* as "a cautionary tale calculated to awaken the university from its dogmatic slumber."[18] He bitterly attacks academia for refusing to open its doors to Benjamin, who, he reminds us, had told Scholem that he had "a thousand reasons" for not wanting to be an academic. In any case, Benjamin is reported to have said, he would have begun by asking for a leave of absence.[19] Wohlfarth further reminds us that Benjamin speaks of an "artistic career" for the bourgeois artist as something which should be interrupted in the service of the revolution.[20] None of this means that Benjamin wouldn't have liked to give academia a try, Wohlfarth assures us, but he could not do so "except on his own terms." Wohlfarth's essay alludes to the difficulties inherent in careerism, professionalism, and academic small-mindedness, all of which are at play in the consider-

16. "Walter Benjamin and His Angel," in Smith, *On Walter Benjamin,* p. 87, n. 15. Scholem says that, according to Benjamin's reading list, he read the "Eighteenth Brumaire" only in 1938, and had only read *Class Struggles in France* before that, in 1928. For a new look at the angel in the triangled context of Scholem, Kafka, and Benjamin, see Robert Alter's elegant study, *Necessary Angels* (Cambridge, MA, 1991).

17. Walter Benjamin, *Understanding Brecht,* trans. Anna Bostock (London, 1988), p. vii.

18. "Resentment Begins at Home," in *On Walter Benjamin,* p. 235.

19. Wohlfarth, *On Benjamin,* p. 258, n. 51.

20. Wohlfarth, in *Reflections,* p. 191.

ation of Benjamin's life. The essay culminates with a footnote (*Benjamin,* 259, n. 52) suggesting that Benjamin's bid for the *Habilitation* was sabotaged by his friend Horkheimer at the last (but crucial) moment. In other words, Benjamin should somehow have been an academic, deserved to be one, was willing to be one (except for the initial leave of absence, which, given our present discussion on sloth, cannot help but amuse in this context), but got betrayed by his friend.[21]

Academia has a peculiar role to play in the essay by Wohlfarth, himself a professor of comparative literature, and one of the most important Benjamin scholars today. Wohlfarth cites Benjamin's passage describing Professor Schultz, "on whose good offices official acceptance of [Benjamin's *Habilitation*] depended." He then adds, "Academic politics with a vengeance! Professor Schultz—or *homo academicus! Homo Academicus*—or *der Mensch des Ressentiments!*" (230). The careerist stakes are finally as high and personal as they were with Adorno and Arendt but more overtly so: Wohlfarth is writing in the late 1980s, so he can add two postscripts to his essay. The second in particular shows a clear discomfort; a kind of self-reappraisal which bathes in Freudian auto-analysis:

> The academic mill grinds slowly. The above text, written in the heat of the moment, is coldly going to press three years later. Its author, on rereading it, is somewhat uneasy with its apocalyptic tone, its anti-institutional mimicry. To brandish good, epic fathers in order to belittle the bad ones down the hall—does such an Oedipal scenario really point a way out of the psychology of resentment? How free oneself from those ghostly fathers without simply reincarnating those one set out to depose? Shades of 1968 . . . (252; Wohlfarth's ellipses)

Shades of 1968? Wohlfarth, after confessing that some of his "genuinely thoughtful" colleagues have of late begun to wonder

21. On the other hand, it was Horkheimer who secured Benjamin the entry visa to the United States. It should be added that Benjamin frequently flirted with academic posts. In 1927, for example, when he thought he would devote himself to learning Hebrew, he spoke with Scholem and Judah Magnes, chancellor of the Hebrew University, about taking on a faculty position at the new school of humanities at that university. He was made a member of the Institut für Sozialforschung in 1935 (thanks in large part to Adorno) and received the small (but regular) amount of money provided by that membership.

whether "Benjamin's work was ever really *intended* for academic acceptance," decides that "perhaps, indeed, it is time to cool it for a while as we search for other alternatives" (253). We should try to see what the university is without "waxing either apocalyptic or defensive on the subject." This may be, he concludes, the best chance "we academics have" to get out of our "mutual resentments."

What all of this comes down to, then, for Wohlfarth and, I would argue, Adorno, Arendt, Horkheimer—the generation just younger than Benjamin—is the status of the *homo academicus* and the entangled politics of resentment generated by a thinker (or is it scholar?) who either refuses to join, or is barred from so doing, the club; whose texts do not fit the academic taxonomics; and who finds the call to the labor force "unspeakable."[22]

In his introduction to *Reflections,* Peter Demetz explains it all this way: "In many Jewish families of late nineteenth-century Europe, gifted sons turned against the commercial interests of their fathers, who were largely assimilated . . . In building their counterworlds in spiritual protest, they incisively shaped the future of science, philosophy, and literature" (ix). This statement is reminiscent of Arendt's own assessment: "Moreover, in his attitude to financial problems Benjamin was by no means an isolated case. If anything, his outlook was typical of an entire generation of German-Jewish intellectuals," although "no one else fared so badly with it" (*Illuminations,* 26). Later, Arendt claims that Benjamin adopted a radical position against "the literary as well as the academic establishment" without suspecting "what isolation and loneliness" such a position would cause (34). The Demetz and Arendt voices merge here perhaps because Demetz is writing the introduction instead of Arendt, who died before the volume was published. She had collected a new series of Benjamin essays to be presented to the American reader, and Demetz is imagining the introduction she might have written. More ghostly fathers; more problems with the famous indolence. "As a young man,"

---

22. Kant was the first philosopher in Germany to become a professor, a tradition in which Arendt and Adorno clearly remained, and in which Benjamin just as clearly did not.

writes Demetz, Benjamin "may have loitered near the railway stations." His interest in the red light districts "may be emblematic of the most secret bents of his mind" (xviii). We will return to these "secret bents."

It is no coincidence that both Arendt and Adorno are the great theoreticians of work. I contend that their assessment of Benjamin is generated not only by what Wohlfarth calls the politics of resentment. ("Resentment Begins at Home" is an interesting title, since nobody in the early, refugee generation of Benjamin scholarship is "at home" *except*—and this may be the point—at the academy.) It is also generated by what I earlier called the work ethic, which is an unquestioned principle within the Marxist critiques of Benjamin we have considered. Like the vestigial tail on the human species, the work ethic remains as a bourgeois given. As Hannah Arendt puts it in *The Human Condition,* work, action, and labor "are fundamental because each corresponds to one of the basic conditions under which life on earth has been given to man" (7).

In *The Human Condition,* Arendt devotes a long footnote to laziness, the positioning of which is significant. (Derrida's demarginalization of footnotes was as yet unwritten, so I can safely say that in placing laziness in a footnote, Arendt is putting the problem of sloth in parentheses.) Arendt discusses laziness within the context of a distinction between labor and work: labor "remains a verbal noun" unrelated to product, whereas work is connected with the product. The footnote gives us another distinction, this one from ancient Greece and Aristotle, between laziness (*aergia*) and *scholē,* "abstention from certain activities which is the condition for a political life" (82, n. 7). "Laziness," Arendt explains, "had the same connotations it has for us" (which are what?), whereas "a life of *scholē* was not considered to be a lazy life." When *scholē* becomes equated with idleness, she continues, that is a development within the *polis.* Xenophon writes that Socrates is accused of instilling a "slavish spirit" in his students because he quoted a line from Hesiod, "Work is no disgrace, but laziness [*aergia*] is a disgrace." Arendt reminds us that there was an earlier "more original, and more general contempt for activities which serve only to sustain life . . . The *opera servilia* are still defined in the eighteenth century."[23]

But in the world of Homer, even menial work is not seen as sordid if it allows for self-sufficiency. So, for example, Paris and Odysseus help build their houses, while "Nausicaa herself washes the linen of her brothers, etc." (83) I am reading the "etc." to mean that this sort of gendered division of labor is consonant with what Arendt refers to as "reality." This is precisely the logic dictating the pathologist Brouardel's remark, cited by Freud, and which I alluded to in the preceding chapter: "Dirty knees are the sign of an honest girl." Arendt's "etc." is an unknowing confirmation of the continuity of such a tradition: building your own house shows self-sufficiency if you are a man. Is washing your brothers' dirty linen also meant to show self-sufficiency in Nausicaa?

One way of getting at the tenor of all of this is to consider the possibility that what is at stake in academic debates concerning Benjamin has changed little from Arendt's depiction of Ancient Greece. Benjamin criticism perhaps demonstrates that the notions of *aergia* and *scholē* not only are still with us but are precisely what is at play in assessments of Benjamin. Is he living a life of laziness, *aergia*, refusing to work and thus to gain self-sufficiency, dependent first on his father and remaining what Demetz calls "the reluctant bourgeois son who has been living on the financial resources of his father" (*Reflections*, xviii), then on friends or benefactors? After all, he practiced and studied (and wrote about) the art of writing from the coffeehouse, writing as surgery (e.g., "Polyclinic" in *One Way Street*), thus openly emulating the text Engels called "a masterpiece of dialectics," Diderot's *Le Neveu de Rameau*.

It is worth rehearsing some of the givens in that well-known

23. On the problem of work and leisure as understood by the ancients, see Joseph Pieper's famous work, *Leisure, the Basis of Culture* (London, 1962). See also André Gorz, *Paths to Paradise: On the Liberation from Work* (Boston, 1985). The important work of Siegfried Kracauer should also be noted with respect to analyzing the place of leisure in daily life (he was also friends with both Benjamin and Adorno). See his *Das Ornament der Masse,* (Frankfurt a.M., 1963) and the forthcoming English translation, *The Mass Ornament*, trans. Thomas Y. Levin (Cambridge, MA, 1993). See also Edith Wyschogrod, *Saints and Postmodernism: Revisioning Moral Philosophy* (Chicago, 1990), pp. 73–86.

text because it is seen as the place where the flâneur's ancestor makes one of his first appearances. In *Rameau's Nephew,* Diderot attempts to understand the strange new breed that has crept up with the establishment of the café. Compared to the rarified, by-invitation-only interiors of the literary salon, the coffee-house presents an open-air atmosphere (which, like the arcades themselves, blur private/public, interior/exterior distinctions). *Bienséance* and the ossified rules of salon wit give way to a more apparently egalitarian debate society (within the confines of those who can afford to loiter, or who have nothing to lose in so doing, which is not the same thing)—anyone can break into the discussion.[24] The *moi* in Diderot's text is shocked by the emer-gence of a creature who has no purpose in life save the observing of other people with a concomitant mooching off them. On the other hand (as if in anticipation of Hegel's ability to turn dialectics upside down), the *lui* asks *moi* if he too is wasting time in coffee-houses with do-nothings (*fainéants*), "pushing wood" (*pousser le bois*). *Moi* answers, "No. But when I have nothing better to do, I amuse myself a bit by watching those who push it well."[25] In other words, the answer to the question is really yes, but since the philosopher (*monsieur le philosophe,* as the nephew sneeringly calls him) is learned and the nephew claims to be ignorant (he professes never to have learned a thing and to be the better off

24. It was, of course, an all-male club, which is another way in which the coffeehouse differs from the literary salon, traditionally both controlled and domi-nated by women. See Janet Wolff's "The Invisible *Flâneuse:* Women and the Liter-ature of Modernity," *Canadian Journal of Political and Social Theory* 2, no. 3, Special Themes 1984/85 (1985): 37–46. Reprinted in a useful book, *The Problems of Moder-nity: Adorno and Benjamin,* ed. Andrew Benjamin (London and New York, 1989). For an excellent study on the role and development of the dandy, see Domna C. Stanton's *The Aristocrat as Art: A Study of the Honnête Homme and the Dandy in Seven-teenth- and Nineteenth-Century France* (New York, 1980). For a book which looks at what happened to the dandy after Oscar Wilde in England (and which looks at the English Renaissance as well), see Richard Pine, *The Dandy and the Herald: Man-ners, Mind and Morals from Brummell to Durrell* (New York, 1988). See also Ellen Moers, *The Dandy: Brummell to Beerbohm* (Lincoln, NE, 1960). Finally, see Susan Buck-Morss, "The Flâneur, the Sandwichman and the Whore: the Politics of Loi-tering," *New German Critique,* no. 39, 2d special issue on Walter Benjamin (fall 1986): 99–139.

25. Diderot, *Oeuvres romanesques* (Paris, 1959), p. 398, (my translation). "Non, mais quand je n'ai rien de mieux à faire, je m'amuse à regarder un instant ceux qui le poussent bien." *Pousser le bois* is an idiomatic expression of the period, meaning playing chess or checkers, the two games that dominated coffeehouses.

for it), *moi* is observing while *lui* is loitering. This irony, of which
the text is well aware, is lacking in most Benjamin studies.

The ease with which Adorno, Arendt, and others are able to
stand on what passes for high moral ground in their view of Benjamin betrays something more than the self-righteousness of or-
thodoxy, something more, even, than the self-satisfaction of the
employed in a work-ethic metaphysics (so pervasive that it permeates everything to the point of becoming invisible), something
more than the academic's constant anxiety that "real" genius
lives outside of its halls and meetings (such that it is constantly
"biting the hand that feeds it," as Wohlfarth puts it to make a
different point). In what we loosely refer to as Western culture,
work is inextricably tied to the notion of identity. The connection
already appears in the Church fathers (acedia prevents you from
doing your duty, thus from participating in the divine good, in
allowing the full development of the soul). It is clearly in Hegel:
the slave in that dialectic ultimately becomes the master because
he *produces;* while the master, who can only consume, becomes
prey to melancholy. "Through work," we read in Hegel, "the
bondsman becomes conscious of what he truly is." While the lord
has only the fleeting victory of recognition which lacks "the side
of objectivity and permanence," the slave has work which "is desire held in check, fleetingness staved off."[26] Later in the *Phenomenology* we read, "The work produced is the reality which consciousness gives itself." The work is perishable, but its activity
allows consciousness to grasp the distinction between doing and
being.

More practically, in Locke's *Treatises on Government,* which we
have been turning to throughout this study, we have a text that
establishes the claim that the work of a man (*sic*) belongs to him.
More significantly, work actually allows for a man to become a
person, precisely by virtue of owning what he has produced. Thus
the first modern (legal) formulation of the notion of person is
grounded in work—labor of the body, work of the hand.

It is perhaps in Marx that we have the most telling passages
of the extent to which work determines "man's" essence (in the

---

26. Hegel, *Phenomenology of Spirit,* trans. A. V. Miller (Oxford, 1977), p. 118.

Sartrean sense). Labor first satisfies the need to "maintain the physical existence." Work (activity) is also "the life of the species." Free and conscious activity is "man's species character." So true is this for Marx that estranged labor alienates man's own body from himself; moreover, it estranges his "spiritual essence, his *human* being."[27] For Marx, echoing both Locke and Hegel, an unnatural relation to work estranges man from his body, from other men, and from his human essence. Estranged labor destroys man's personhood, consciousness, human-beingness, by degrading activity into a means. Free, spontaneous labor, on the other hand, allows man to "contemplate himself in a world that he has created."

According to Michel Foucault, although idleness is a sin in both Catholic and Protestant dogma, it is with Calvin that sloth assumes a certain pretentiousness, "the absurd pride of poverty."

> If it is true that labor is not inscribed among the laws of nature, it is enveloped in the order of the fallen world. This is why idleness is rebellion—the worst form of all, in a sense: it waits for nature to be generous as in the innocence of Eden, and seeks to constrain a Goodness to which man cannot lay claim since Adam. Pride was the sin of man before the Fall; but the sin of idleness is the supreme pride of man once he has fallen, the absurd pride of poverty.[28]

The reason labor enters houses of confinement in the Age of Reason, Foucault argues, is that "since sloth had become the absolute form of rebellion, the idle would be forced to work, in the endless leisure of a labor without utility or profit" (*Madness,* 57). Thus economic and moral ideologies join to create a labor/idleness demarcation, allowing for exclusionary doctrines of varying sorts. We find this demarcation echoed in Locke, Hegel, and Marx, and continuing in phrases such as Arendt's explanation of the category into which she finally classifies Benjamin (having earlier grouped him with the "unclassifiable ones"): the *homme de lettres,* a prerevolutionary figure in France. Men such as these, Arendt writes,

27. *The Marx-Engels Reader,* ed. Robert C. Tucker (New York, 1978), pp. 76–77.
28. Michel Foucault, *Madness and Civilization: A History of Insanity in the Age of Reason,* trans. Richard Howard (New York, 1965), p. 56.

were neither obliged nor willing to write and read professionally, in order to earn a living. Unlike the class of the intellectuals, who offer their services either to the state as experts, specialists, and officials, or to society for diversion and instruction, the *hommes de lettres* always strove to keep aloof from both the state and society. Their material existence was based on income without work, and their intellectual attitude rested upon their resolute refusal to be integrated politically or socially. (*Illuminations,* 27)

Benjamin, Arendt assures us, is a throwback to this figure; it is "the only 'position' for which he was born." Benjamin, then, is irritating because he has aristocratic pretentions of indolence (a perfectly "legitimate" Marxist complaint). On the other hand, he is equally irritating because he does not grasp the good Calvinist slogan that God only helps those who help themselves. The work ethic, linking, as I have suggested, morality and economics, muddies the discourse.[29]

The other option, if we return to Arendt's discussion, is to argue that Benjamin's life was one not of laziness but of *scholē,* an "abstention from certain activities which is the condition for a political life. Contempt for laboring, originally arising out of a passionate striving for freedom from necessity and a no less passionate impatience with every effort that left no trace, no monument, no great work worthy of remembrance, spread with the increasing demands of *polis* life upon the time of the citizens and its insistence on their abstention from all but political activities, until it covered everything that demanded an effort" (*Human Condition,* p. 81). Hence, not laziness at all, not shirking work; just shirking work that gets in the way of the real work, the *opus magnum.* There are times in the texts of Adorno and Arendt, and of the others cited here, when Benjamin's life is seen as one of *scholē*—a necessary, even courageous withdrawal from the world for the sake of observing modernity, for writing the city.

But Adorno quickly reminds us of the absence of the *polis* in

29. Weber, citing the *Christian Directory* in a footnote, sees the move from the will of God to the "purely utilitarian view-point of the later liberal theory" in the statement that "work is the moral as well as the natural end of power . . . The public welfare or the good of the many is to be valued above our own." *The Protestant Ethic and the Spirit of Capitalism,* p. 260, n. 9). This later argument actually blurs the *aergia/skhole* distinction, since a life of activity is seen as necessary to the good of the many.

Benjamin's life: He has "the weakness of an isolated individual," for "private reflection is deficient as long as it is separated from social movements and praxis that aim at changing the situation."[30] You cannot claim to be a Marxist and simultaneously join the Action Française, as Benjamin did to protest the German political scene. There are moments in some of these Benjamin critiques in which he is cast in the role of a Judas: he is willing to betray what is most sacred (in this case, political conviction and *engagement*) for money. Here is Arendt again: "In order to receive [a monthly stipend] after his parents' death [Benjamin] was ready, or thought he was, to do many things: to study Hebrew for three hundred marks a month if the Zionists thought it would do them some good, or to think dialectically, with all the mediating trimmings, for one thousand French francs if there was no other way of doing business with the Marxists. The fact that despite being down and out he later did neither is worthy of admiration" (*Illuminations,* 27). The bone she throws Benjamin at the end of this passage notwithstanding, Arendt keeps rocking back and forth between Calvinist/Marxist rage at Benjamin's indolence/aristocratic fopisms on the one hand, and horror at his willingness to sell out for an income on the other. The point I wish to stress, however, is that problematizing Benjamin's relation to work makes possible a complex constellation (to use his term): one which depicts him as politically naive and at times unreliable; which characterizes his texts as eccentric and inconsistent (if brilliant); which domesticates his observations of modernity by eliding him with a textual economy of *flânerie;* which genders his gait (both as a pedestrian and writer) so that his originality, by virtue of being placed in the economy of a typed "femininity," is always somehow in question. "His capacity for continually bringing out new aspects . . . can hardly be adequately described by the concept of 'originality' . . . The metaphor of creator is thoroughly inappropriate for him" (Adorno, *Prisms,* 229).

Benjamin's notes show that he had planned to study the concept of sloth (indolence) in his unfinished *Paris, Capital of the Nine-*

30. Introduction, in Walter Benjamin, *Gesammelte Schriften,* ed. Rolf Tiedemann and Hermann Schweppenhäuser, 7 vols. in 14 (Frankfurt a.M., 1972–89), 1:15.

teenth Century.[31] He saw it as a symptom of modernity (mental distraction and hyperstimulation being others). Certainly we could have used his study, as the critical assumptions of many Benjamin scholars more than amply demonstrate.[32] Indolence, laziness, sloth, *aergia*—these variants for what Benjamin calls acedia house a complex of assumptions concerning everything from the moral duty of "man" in relation to the polis, to the debilitating and fascinating effects of city life upon the species, to the right and wrong way of writing history itself.

If, as Weber and others point out, acedia interferes with the methodical life, with the move from agrarian rhythms to commercial time by clocks, with the dictum that the useful life is the productive life (where product is measured in goods), it is precisely for this reason that Benjamin favors that cardinal "sin." In a move that reverses the gendering (feminization) leveled against his texts, Benjamin equates clock time with "historicism's bordello" where the main whore is called "Once upon a time" (*Illuminations,* 262). On the other hand, the historical materialist "remains in control of his powers, man enough to blast open the continuum of history." For Benjamin, real progress is not "in the continuity of the flow of time," not linearity or clock time. It is rather "in its interferences: wherever something genuinely new makes itself felt for the first time with the sobriety of dawn."[33] "Once upon a time" is nothing more than fate draped as progress, as Habermas remarked in another context.

To be "man enough" to blast open the continuum of history? The gendering of modernity has become an endless debate of late,[34] but let it be noted here that Benjamin himself gestures to-

31. Benjamin, *Das Passagen-Werk,* in *Gesammelte Schriften,* 5/2:962.
32. One work that persuasively and forcefully undertakes such a study, inspired by Benjamin's unwritten indolence chapter, is Anson Rabinbach's *The Human Motor: Energy, Fatigue, and the Origins of Modernity* (Berkeley and Los Angeles, 1990).
33. In Rolf Tiedemann, who is citing from the Arcades Project, *Studien zur Philosophie Walter Benjamins* (Frankfurt a.M., 1965), p. 103.
34. e.g., Christine Buci-Glucksman, "Catastrophic Utopia: The Feminine as Allegory of the Modern," *Representations* 14 (spring 1986); Marshall Bermann, *All That Is Solid Melts into Air: The Experience of Modernity* (London, 1983); Janet Wolff, "The Invisible Flâneuse"; Buck-Morss, "The Flâneur, the Sandwichman and the Whore"; Angelika Rauch, "The *Trauerspiel* of the Prostituted Body, or Woman as Allegory of Modernity," *Cultural Critique,* Fall 1988, pp. 77–88, which directly

ward the feminine when he speaks of his writing: he sees his failed *Habilitationschrift* as a Sleeping Beauty and compares books to prostitutes. More importantly, he places himself in a willfully complex situation vis-à-vis originality itself, thus occluding the masculinist insistence on author as creator, as innovator (an insistence maintained by his critics, as we have seen).

Origin itself, Benjamin claimed, "has nothing to do with beginnings." Its "rhythm is apparent only to a double insight."[35] The full title of the *Habilitation* thesis begins with "The Origin" (*Ursprung*), but is to be understood as "that which emerges out of the process of becoming and disappearing," not beginnings. His ideal was a book which would eliminate all commentary and consist of nothing but quotations: "Method of this project: literary montage. I have nothing to say. I have only to show. I will neither misappropriate anything worthwhile nor annex to myself any brilliant formulations."[36] Text as parthenogenesis is a notion that Benjamin rejects from the start, not only by refuting what he called "novelty" but also by having as his highest ambition the writing of a book in which the citations would be presented unmediated by an authorial commentary (unannexed).

It was a book of quotations which, like *Le Livre* of Mallarmé, was never to be written; but its position in the Benjamin *oeuvre* is no less idealized. It would have similarly erased the voice of the author, although with a different agenda. It would, by its very patchwork structure, have achieved the *chiffonier*'s work Benjamin so admired;[37] and by the same token, it would have elimi-

takes on the relation of Benjamin to prostitution. See also Andreas Huyssen, "The Vamp and the Machine," in *After the Great Divide* (see above, chap. 2, n. 10); Alice Jardine, *Gynesis: Configurations of Gender and Modernity* (Ithaca, NY, 1985). This is just a sampling of the discussion.

35. From a letter to Scholem, 23 April 1928. These lines open Susan Buck-Morss's magnificent study, *The Dialectics of Seeing: Walter Benjamin and the Arcades Project* (Cambridge, MA, 1991), p. 9.

36. *Gesammelte Schriften,* 5/1a:8. It is unclear whether this project was literally to comprise only quotations; Adorno thinks yes, Tiedemann no. *Über Walter Benjamin,* p. 26. See also Tiedemann's introduction to the *Passagen-Werk,* in *Gesammelte Schriften* 5/2.

37. Stendhal uses a similar metaphor to describe his "own" work on Metastase. Citing Fénelon, Stendhal adds, "Not all of the stolen ideas have been written down with exactitude. This brochure is almost nothing but a centon." *Vie de Haydn* . . . , p. 395, n. 1. This is one of the two passages Rolland sees as admitting some guilt for the plagiarisms. A *centon,* says the Larousse, is from the Latin *cento,* and

nated linearity, clock time, origins as beginnings, the privileged status of author vis-à-vis originality. Instead we have the great (incomplete, incompletable) achievement of the Arcades Project.

The various texts on Benjamin considered here are only a small part of what now constitutes a veritable Benjamin industry. But as much as the texts of this industry address the importance and complexity of Benjamin, they also demonstrate the urgency of the mythology of originality. It is an urgency that may in fact be inextricable from the study of literature and literary criticism, if only because originality helps define the modern notion of author and of what is regarded as new, even though such concepts are put into question. But just as the critical establishment reserves for itself the right to judge and canonize texts, it in turn produces its own original narrative, its own claims to newness and discovery. Beneath the arguments over the textual flâneries of Benjamin lies a struggle to protect the narrative of originality, as well as the critical discourse it both protects and produces.

---

in French is a "piece of verse or prose, made up of fragments borrowed from diverse authors." The *Oxford Latin Dictionary* says that a *cento* is "a quilt, blanket or curtain made of old garments stitched together." *Centonism,* says Webster's, is "the act or practice of arranging borrowed literary, artistic, or musical features in a new order, thus forming a patchwork composition." Thus the centonism that Stendhal practiced surreptitiously is what Benjamin calls for as a new practice of writing. Stendhal's quilt becomes Benjamin's ragpicker, and the former's stitching becomes the latter's *bricolage* before the fact.

CONCLUSION

ROLAND BARTHES has remarked that the unity of a text is not in its origin but in its destination.[1] Or, invoking Lacan's terminology, we might say that origin and its product, originality, form a system of desire that is endlessly displaced. Displacement itself, not to mention the discourse of desire, is signposted as feminine in the Western tradition. Freud's chain of somatic symptoms form the topography of hysteria: an origin of the species personified as the womb displaces itself, literalizing the tradition. Nietzsche feminizes the displacing dance of truth and the place of truth itself, a move which Derrida, for example, comments upon and in so doing repeats even as he attempts to extract himself. These writers partake of the same economy of displacement, a motif of the emperor and his new clothes, that has been amply analyzed by critical theory. Indeed, displacement as a trope or strategy (or both) has become a critical commonplace, so that it is easy to overlook how specifically gendered it remains in all of its variants.

The hypothesis put forward in the present book is that the literary mythology of originality participates in the same economy of displacement. Originality is variously displaced to clothe its status as invention, or as myth, necessary for the culture industry it supports: the dual production of literature and the author, and its curator—the figure of the critic himself. The critic is "the pioneer of education and the shaper of cultural tradition," claims Northrop Frye. More ominously, a public that tries to do without criticism, and asserts that it knows what it wants or likes, "brutalizes the arts and loses its cultural memory." Whereas "all the arts are dumb," Frye concludes, echoing Plato, "criticism can talk."[2]

And talk, as we know, it does. I have turned to the grand old

---

1. Barthes, *The Rustle of Language,* trans. Richard Howard (New York, 1986), pp. 50–52.
2. Frye, *Anatomy of Criticism* (New York, 1969), p. 4.

text of the *Anatomy of Criticism* and to its self-avowed "Polemical Introduction" because it shows its hand with pride: criticism judges, then canonizes or exiles. Criticism is the museum of culture and the critic, educator of "the public." The critic's originality lies in his[3] ability to detect and demarcate an origin, and then to articulate its boundaries. But if the critic preserves culture's memory and the parameters of taste for a given age, there seems to be a critical unconscious at work as well, one which continues, even if covertly, to fashion critical assumptions about reading and judging texts. Frye's postulates are not so much out-of-date as they are baldly straightforward and unapologetic.

Most current theory sees the modern author as a consequence of those things which led to the foregrounding of the individual: French rationalism, British empiricism, the Enlightenment, the Reformation, and the Italian Renaissance. I would add that the role of the critic rests upon, and even adds to, the prestige of the subject; yet at the same time (as I have tried to point out in these pages) he may go about dismantling the very notion of subjectivity. Literary criticism is an institution that proves Adorno's point: the culture industry allows the new always to occur, but as suspected copy.

At least since the nineteenth century, it has been the critic's self-appointed, if unacknowledged (unconscious) task to cull the real new from the false, to identify the point of origin and thus to recognize genuine originality. I submit that this continues to be the critic's understanding of his or her role. Not much has changed since the pronouncements of Northrop Frye. It is part of criticism's system of self-promotion and self-preservation to produce ironic textual smiles, which are intended to indicate that things *have* changed, that criticism has progressed far beyond its former versions—even, and maybe especially, when the critic is accusing others of precisely such a démarche.

The present book is (alas!) no exception. The criticism which claims that there is no such thing as originality is collaborating in the same system of belief, if only by presuming a fresh view on

---

3. Here, as in the rest of this study, the pronouns are intentionally gendered, depending upon the context and agenda as I understand them.

an old problem. What Derrida said of psychoanalysis, I contend is true of criticism: once it invents itself, it finds itself everywhere, even if its major purpose is to deny its own claims. Originality remains a major requirement for criticism, first for the literary texts it professes to judge, but also (although this remains mostly unacknowledged) for itself, a move which allows for the dismissal, for example, of other kinds of criticism or theory (such moves are more commonly made against theories than against fiction). Hence the eternal chain of displaced desire. Critical texts, much like philosophical ones, leapfrog over each other, redefining the previous terms in what is purported to be a new way. While one might (properly) think of Harold Bloom's *Anxiety of Influence* here, the claims in the present book are differently oriented. The anxiety of being influenced (the oedipal problem and so on) is but one symptom within the larger systemic disorder that I have called a metaphysics of origin.

The gendering of origin (and thus of originality), as I hope this study has succeeded in arguing, is a more specific facet of the problem. The prose of hysteria emerges not only from what is understood to be a feminized position; it also stems from the same patriarchal system that seeks to objectify all that is feminine and to feminize all that it sees as objectionable. We might say that the insistence upon originality, and the displacements such an insistence entails, reveal gynophobia in the text of Western literature. An overt gynophobia clothes the desire to be female; the fear of being feminized covers the fear of wishing to be so. A series of possible questions spring almost randomly to mind—for example, Is the emperor naked or in drag? What kind of clothing is covering Nietzsche's truth? Is Freud onto something when he insists that a woman's baby substitutes for her lack of penis, or is it exactly the other way around? Does the point of origin gender the signifier and all those swept in its path, as Lacan claims? Then why, if that point of origin is male gendered, are its movements caught in a web of imaginary male femininity?

Indeed, the story of Adam and Eve can be read as an elaborate obfuscation of the originator of original sin: Eve, the Prometheus turned woman, who takes the initiative, becomes merely the more gullible (bored, indolent) tool of the male serpent. The gendering of indolence is oddly connected with the gendering of a metaphysics of origin. As Froma Zeitlin notes, Hesiod's Pandora is a marvelous tale of punishing initiative, and of repressing female invention. Woman is insisted upon as supplemental, as secondary to any task, and as destructive to the world when she takes matters into her own hands. If she is linked to any originality, it is in that of (ignorantly) unleashing evil, or of preventing man from creating what is good. Significantly, in the *Theogony,* Hesiod describes his brother as an idle consumer, a useless parasite who, like a woman or a drone, merely buzzes. He is feminized, notes Zeitlin, precisely on the grounds of his indolence: since he neither works nor innovates, he is womanly.[4]

Certainly the equation of woman = lack of real work and of originality is how I have read Colette's fight for authorship and a certain aspect of the reception of Benjamin's flâneur. But the equation also offers one way of reading Freud's dream of being first. Freud is fascinated and, I think, identifies with a Descartes who is feminized (rendered indolent—even, it will be recalled, allowed to sleep late in the morning at school) by his mother's ill health and cough until he gives birth (with travail, in his bed, at night) to his dreams and thus to a new self and its (original) philosophy. So Freud will feel that he does not exist until he "invents" psychoanalysis and is thus able to escape the indolence which is the hallmark both of women and of their effect upon men. It was his fiancée Martha, after all, who called him away from his cocaine research and thus was the cause, Freud was convinced, of an original discovery slipping through his fingers.

This same logic, it will be recalled, will later serve to articulate the argument of *Civilization and Its Discontents:* because they are closer to nature (and already, as it were, castrated), women take men away from the task at hand, and slow the process of civilization, to which they are only obliquely related. In another curious instance in which the "authors" and certain obsessive mytholo-

4. Froma Zeitlin, "The Case of Hesiod's Pandora," unpublished as of this printing. Zeitlin also makes the fascinating point that Pandora's "jar," as described by Hesiod, looks like an upside-down uterus, an image that might almost serve as the icon for the points I am attempting to stress here.

gies (as Charles Mauron would have put it) continue to intersect in the present study, Walter Benjamin went to interview the "female artist" (*Künstlerin*) Colette during his exile in Paris. The short piece that resulted from this encounter is called "Should Women Take Part in Political Life? Against: The Poetess [Dichterin] Colette." Women, said Colette to her nervous interlocutor, should never serve on juries or take part in any political activity because they menstruate. Even the most intelligent, self-possessed and well-educated women, she says, have at least two or three days every month when they are overexcited and out of control. She prefaces these remarks by assuring Benjamin that she herself is past the age of such hormonal upheavals (thus professing to validate her discourse thereupon). It is impossible to tell whether Colette (who, it will be remembered, was no feminist) is pulling Benjamin's leg or not: he is a cautious but uncertain narrator of the encounter.

Colette looks at Benjamin with a glance that he calls hard to define, and waits for him to speak. But he has no intention, he tells us, of advocating such positions—positions nearly identical to Freud's but which a great woman author seems to be espousing. Benjamin, the refugee who is struggling through a highly nuanced rhetoric in a language not his own, concludes that Colette is "very smart, very precise and very French," and that she resembles the creatures, human and otherwise, that she has "so truly and bitterly" depicted for us.

If Adorno and Celan's failure to meet in the mountains helped to inspire Celan's essay about a conversation where "the Jew" meets himself, Benjamin's delicate, almost tongue-in-cheek description of his conversation with Colette seems to enact the cliché of Woman-as-Enigma from the "male" perspective. He can't tell if he is being had; the conversation is interesting, but clearly a failure. The ground is not common when the issue is gender: Is Colette distancing herself from women or from the male version of them?[5] It is a measure of the extent to which femininity is understood as profoundly nonlogical, as very much given to tem-

---

5. Walter Benjamin, *Gesammelte Schriften,* 4/1, 2:492–95.

porary bouts of madness, that the tenor of Colette's assertions remains unclear—to Benjamin, and consequently, to his reader. The female author is a kind of monster.

Let us return to the curious coupling of femininity and Jewishness with respect to the "indolence = feminine" equation. *Über die letzten Dingen* (1904), a work by Otto Weiniger (a "self-hating Jew," as he was known), contains a passage which links Jews to indolence, or a lack of productivity. The passage—one of many in Weiniger to make such an argument—if considered from the perspective on indolence which I have been proposing, reveals the tortuous logic leading to the kinship Weiniger establishes between Jewishness and femininity: "The Jew will not burden himself with responsibility (and for this reason avoids problems); he is thus unproductive. The only obligation he has is . . . to avoid purpose and the demands of life."[6] The word "woman" could just as easily be substituted for "Jew." Indeed, Weiniger's popular *Geschlecht und Charakter* (also 1904) specifically argues a racial anthropology based on "protoplasm," which is said to produce strong or weak individuals, depending on the amount. Jews, like women (and homosexuals), wrote Weiniger, were among the weak; rootless, they lacked what he called "character."

The rhetoric found in Weiniger's passage—which labels "the Jew" as refusing responsibility, as "unproductive," avoiding the "purpose and demands of life," and (elsewhere) as parasitic of society—resurfaces in the more refined prose of Arendt and Adorno, in their assessment of Benjamin. The anti-Semitism (self-hating or not) lurking within such prose goes hand in hand with a certain misogyny, a relation explicit in the Weiniger text.[7]

When I argue for the gendering of origin, and for the search for originality as an endless, hysterical symptom of displacement, I am not partaking of the present interest in the "gender of modernity." Rather, I am suggesting that the way in which gender is imagined, and femininity in particular is inscribed, in the ontol-

---

6. Weiniger, *Über die letzten Dingen* (Vienna, 1903). Cited by Dennis B. Klein, in *Jewish Origins of the Psychoanalytic Movement* (Chicago, 1985), p. 118.

7. Such a claim is hardly uncommon at the turn of the century. Otto Rank, the writer who was to become a psychoanalyst, wrote in his journal that the Jews were essentially a "lazy" people because they were petty and restless. Cited by Klein in *Jewish Origins of Psychoanalysis*, p. 110.

ogy of the European text is a central aspect of the metaphysics of origin.

Points of origin naturally exclude, and it is in a historical, political context of exclusion that I have been using "displacement." I have used the term as a metaphor (at times with psychoanalytic, Lacanian, and linguistic overtones), but I also mean it topographically: displacement as deterritorialization, or/and as the loss of private property. In this sense, Celan, Adorno, Arendt, and Benjamin share the rift from a given place of origin. The way in which they confront the failure of philosophy in the face of the Holocaust, the way in which they do or do not see language as necessarily collaborative after the Holocaust, the extent to which they participate or not in a reconstitution of a homeland and in the real or imagined parameters of such a homeland—these all serve to differentiate between political and personal stances, within historical limits. But they are also responses, generating a writing that continually retraces the need for origin.

Moreover, if we return to the four names mentioned, there are the specific questions of who survives (Adorno and Arendt do; Benjamin and, ultimately, Celan do not); of the role of European guilt; and of the *place* of the refugee—the displaced person whose point of origin is always unclear (or, conversely, always too clearly un-European). In certain historical moments, terms such as origin and displacement emerge as a fundamental part of the administrative language of immigration, of refugee status and of identity papers (or lack thereof). They are the machinery of political repression, and as such are terms which have the most concrete and irrevocable consequences imaginable for life, for everyday life, and for death. Suffused with the theology of origin, these words provide the state with grounds for exclusion, execution, exile, or internment. The texts we have discussed are fully inscribed with the reality of displacement and origin, which in turn function simultaneously on both a metaphorical and an experiential level. Celan's *no pasarán,* for example, is profoundly not a metaphor.

I hope I have made clear that my argument applies to any minority discourse/dominant culture dialectic, whether determined by race, class, gender, religion, geography, ethnic identification, or other "grouping." The specificity of the historical contexts in the present study has been unavoidably dictated (and properly so, which is my point) by the texts I have examined. And while textual choices are always personally motivated, mine are not meant to be read as partaking in the paradox of "majoritizing" a given marginalized group and thus privileging one minority discourse over another.

I want the terms "displacement" and "origin," then, to be understood as figures of speech that simultaneously possess a political, fatal power. They are both discursive formations (to use Foucault's phrase) and words that literalize themselves. There is a lost *place* in being displaced; a stated point of origin in the metaphysics of origin; a ground to stand upon as a speaking (landed) subject; a spatial and material character to text; specific legal and financial consequences for women to terms such as "naming" and "property."[8] My own text alternates between the rhetorical and political valences of these terms because that is precisely how I am understanding literary language: as grounded in a multivalence that is never innocent, never only rhetorical, never free of the collaborative impulse with respect to origin.

8. And for Jews (to name but one of several ethnic groups this condition describes). Klein points out that Otto Rank had decided, but then hesitated, to change his name to Rank from the original Rosenfeld. He was moved to change it, according to Klein, both because it sounded too Jewish, and because he wanted to repudiate his father. But Austrian law at the time (1908, when Rank first applied to change surnames) held that "an author who did not use a legally recognized name would lose royalties on published material." His request was finally granted, but only upon his conversion to the Catholic faith, in 1909. Klein, *Jewish Origins*, p. 134, n. 28. The double bind is that while naming allows for copyright, the name must be your "own"—an interesting dilemma for marginals such as Jews and women, who at the turn of the century in Europe frequently have trouble owning anything, including their (own) names. Jews, of course, were notoriously disallowed from choosing names, and were also limited to authorized spellings for the names that were permissible. Celan foregrounds this difficulty by turning his name backwards from the "original," which was spelled variously "Antschel," "Anczel," and "Ancel." On the other hand, there is the case of Adorno, who gradually put his father's name (Weisengrund) second and used his Italian mother's name as a surname.

INDEX